PRAISE FOR LAURIE NOTARO

"If Laurie Notaro's books don't inspire pants-wetting fits of laughter, then please consult your physician because clearly your funny bone is broken."

—Jen Lancaster

"Hilarious, fabulously improper, and completely relatable, Notaro is the queen of funny."

—Celia Rivenbark

"Whenever I pick up a book by Laurie Notaro, I know I'll be in a good mood soon. Because Laurie Notaro makes me laugh. Period."

—Meg Cabot

"Pure, unexpurgated Notaro . . . again, she turns on the truth serum and the results are once more riotously funny."

—*San Antonio Express-News*

"For pure laugh-out-loud, then read-out-loud fun, it's hard to beat this humor writer."

—*New Orleans Times-Picayune*

"[Notaro] may be the funniest writer in this solar system."

—*Miami Herald*

EXCUSE ME WHILE I DISAPPEAR

ALSO BY LAURIE NOTARO

We Thought You Would Be Prettier:
True Tales of the Dorkiest Girl Alive

An Idiot Girl's Christmas:
True Tales from the Top of the Naughty List

The Idiot Girl and the Flaming Tantrum of Death:
Reflections on Revenge, Germophobia,
and Laser Hair Removal

It Looked Different on the Model:
Epic Tales of Impending Shame and Infamy

The Potty Mouth at the Table

Enter Pirates: Vintage Legends

Housebroken

Predictably Disastrous Results:
Vintage Legends Volume II

EXCUSE ME WHILE I DISAPPEAR

TALES OF MIDLIFE MAYHEM

LAURIE NOTARO

Little
a

Published by Little A, New York

www.apub.com

Amazon, the Amazon logo, and Little A are trademarks of Amazon.com,
Inc., or its affiliates.

ISBN-13: 9781542033510 (hardcover)
ISBN-10: 1542033519 (hardcover)

ISBN-13: 9781542033503 (paperback)
ISBN-10: 1542033500 (paperback)

Cover design by Shasti O'Leary Soudant

Printed in the United States of America

First edition

To the brightest light of my life, Maeby.
My darling girl, I hope we deserved you,
and that you knew how much we loved you
and will always love you beyond all things
imaginable.
And to my mom, for (not so quietly) suffering
through my entire career. You are mostly
anonymous in this book, but you are the
funniest person on this earth. Own it.

Table of Contents

Girl Gone Gray

"I've decided," I said as I plopped down in the cushy salon chair. "Today is the day."

My hairstylist looked a little shocked, but I nodded. "I'm going all the way."

"Okay," she said. "But you have to be sure. You *really* have to be sure, because there's no going back."

"Full steam ahead!" I tallyhoed. "Make me gray!"

I won't lie. I wasn't a mature woman embracing her true self, age, and root color. I had, instead, recently seen a photo of myself in which someone had clearly poured powdered sugar on my head, right down the part, with the surgical precision of an alien ship leaving crop circles.

"Look at that!" I said to my husband, pointing at the image on Facebook. "Someone was eating a doughnut above my head! Why didn't someone tell me?"

My husband peered over my shoulder, took a good look at me, and quickly said, "I think I hear the teakettle."

Odd, I thought. *I didn't hear a teakettle.* I followed him into the kitchen. He glanced back and picked up his pace, sprinting into the dining room.

"I didn't hear anything," I said as I pursued him through the living room and back to the kitchen. On my second lap, I got a good look at the empty stove.

"There's no teakettle!" I said louder as he doubled back to the dining room, where I found him blocked by Maeby, our Australian shepherd. She'd realized that the sheep had escaped the pen and was now frantically herding my husband into his chair.

"There's no teakettle!" I asserted again.

My husband threw his arms up. "Just as there was no doughnut."

"What?"

"There was no doughnut," he explained. "No one dropped powdered sugar on your head."

"Okay," I said, beginning to laugh. "Maybe it was cocaine."

"One of your friends just got a fellowship at Harvard," he stated. "Another one runs a hedge fund on Wall Street. One owns a bookstore. Another was the president of the PTA in a snooty neighborhood. And don't forget the one fighting malaria in Africa—but, more importantly, Bill Gates knows that one's first *and* last name. No one is doing cocaine at your Scottsdale cinnamon roll french toast brunches."

"Okay!" I said, fully laughing. "I guess it was a bad light reflection."

"It was not a bad light reflection!" my husband finally spouted. "It's your roots. Your roots are *white*."

I squinted at him, unbelieving. "But I get them done every three weeks. At a hundred and seventy dollars a pop. Plus tip. And I'm a good tipper."

"Well, the real tip is that every three weeks, they grow back—white," he said. "Honey, I think you're gray."

There was every possibility that he was right. I'd found my first gray hair at twenty-two, and after that they just kept coming. I'd invested in the occasional box of L'Oréal every now and then for the first twenty years or so. Later, when I was sick of guests inquiring furtively about the brown splotches on the walls of my bathroom—because I apparently rinsed out hair dye as if I were a wet dog—I started getting my hair dyed professionally. At first, I made a trip to the salon every five weeks, and then, as I merged into my forties, every four. Eventually, I worked my way up to a three-week rotation. I knew more about my colorist than I did my therapist and was actually offended when I did not make it onto the guest list for her wedding.

Perhaps I shouldn't have gasped when she mentioned that she was using fake flowers from Michaels to create her centerpieces, or suggested lightly, "Remember, not everyone can pull off a sleeveless dress. It's true. My sister once fired me from her wedding party when I pointed out that the average BMI of her bridesmaids definitely pointed to arm coverings, unless the Spanx lady had suddenly invented a girdle for flesh curtains."

So every three weeks, when I visited my fake-flower-loving colorist for my fake chestnut-brown hair, I was investing $170 plus a good tip into a lie, and it had stopped delivering returns. The way I saw it, I had several options.

Move my coloring appointments to every two weeks, the cost of which would have decimated my snack budget, even though evidence on my colorist's Facebook page revealed—to my aesthetic horror—that the bridal party was indeed sleeveless, despite the fact that photos live forever.

Get a wig. Initially, this seemed like a great idea. Can you imagine putting on your hair like a bra? It would be that easy! Then I actually tried a few on at the mall's wig store and instantly transformed myself into an aged prostitute. Not to mention, those wigs are itchy. I thought about seeking out a higher-end wig, but the idea of finding someone else's hair in my food every time I cooked made me want to hurl on the spot.

Become a hat person. I tried to think of women I knew who wore hats or artfully tied scarves regularly, and the vision wasn't promising, being that their faces were typically covered in new biopsy Band-Aids every week, and most of them rode the bus for free with their senior passes. So, no. It also turns out that I have an enormous head, which explains some of my mother's feelings toward me. She most likely still has several stitches in place from October 1965.

Revert to my birth religion and join the order. This move would have solved my hair problem in a snap, but I wasn't sold on wearing a habit. First there was the question of adopting an entire belief system that I had already rejected at the age of twelve when episodes of *Little House on the Prairie* interfered with my confirmation classes. But I was still considering joining a convent (free food, free rent, walks around long gardens, chastising small children) until I realized that the fabric choices were limited, because the Catholic Church only springs for cotton if you're the pope. If there's something I want less on my head than a gray hair, it's polyester. But the ultimate nail in the coffin of this idea was the realization that there are pins and magnets involved in securing the head covering, and pins anywhere in the relative proximity of my eyes is an instant deal breaker.

Face the truth. I am past fifty. I have gray hair. Big deal. What was I so afraid of? Looking my age? *That's ridiculous*, I thought to myself. I have somehow lived through five decades of bad decisions. I have scars that look like I got them in prison, and none of the under forties I work with believe that mothers used to send their children off with ham and cheese sandwiches in metal lunch boxes in 115-degree heat without one of those children dying. I have beaten the odds! My impressive consumption of cigarettes and Pepsi alone made the State Farm life insurance agent laugh out loud when I was seeking coverage. I am old, but I am alive. If you would have spent only an hour with me in 1993, even if I was sleeping, you would have laughed harder than the State Farm agent at the possibility of my reaching the gray-hair stage of life.

But I made it. I am here. So why not . . . show off a little? I proved them (every one of my mother's friends) wrong; I didn't end up in rehab, prison, or an urn. I'm still alive! I've seen more than half a century of events. I've seen so much stuff that I had to purge 90 percent of my childhood memories from my brain in order to make room for passwords and PINs.

I've realized that nearly every day, I learn something new. That means that, at my age now, I have so much more knowledge and perspective than I did at twenty-seven. I've seen more things, had more experiences, and am honestly smarter than I was thirty years ago. There simply is no arguing with that. At fifty-plus, I now know that:

- You should never trust a junkie, no matter how blue their eyes are.
- When a motorcycle gang member named Pudgy wants to hang out at your house, it's not because he thinks you're cool; it's to scout your living

room for shit he can come back and steal later when you aren't home.

- When you suspect that your boss is a little off and demonstrates multiple personalities, HR is not going to help you, and you need to find another job stat.
- If you need to fart at work, you need to go outside and find an active leaf blower or a steady stream of traffic to serve as a sound buffer.

Why shouldn't I be proud of navigating life up until this point and wearing the badges to prove it? If each gray hair that sprouted from my head could equate to every new thing I've learned (being robbed by Pudgy the Biker gave me at least five hundred), that's pretty much the same as getting a PhD in life without eighty thousand in student loan debt.

Why wouldn't I want to brag about that?

My mother, however, had other opinions when I told her about my decision to let nature take over my head.

"That is a terrible decision," she, whose scalp is so tough after applying 672 solutions of Revlon ColorSilk in Light Ash that I'm thinking about using it as a pot holder after she dies, said immediately. "That's a shame. A daughter who looks older than her mother. Now everyone is going to think I'm old because *you* look so old."

"But don't you think that gray hair is a symbol of knowledge and experience?" I asked, already knowing her answer. "Plus, we can move in together with two of my friends and have a hit sitcom!"

"If you want to look like shit, look like shit," she replied. "I don't know what else to tell you. All I know is that when you use my bathroom, it won't look like a monkey had a fight with another monkey in there. It will just look like a haunted house with all of the disgusting spiderwebs."

My sister had a similar take. "Why would you do that?!" she exclaimed. "It's like you're just giving up."

"Remember when I was thirty-five and put a burgundy tint in my hair, and you said I was an old person trying to look young and that I should just buy a set of bingo cards?" I asked.

"I was not lying," she responded. "But you can't give in so easy!"

"Easy?" I laughed. "A hundred and seventy bucks plus a very good tip every three weeks to sit in a chair and chitchat for two hours with someone who doesn't even invite you to her wedding is not easy. I've put in my time. Investing that time and money is dedication! And it wasn't even working. Do you know that I saw a picture of myself and genuinely thought that someone had eaten a powdered doughnut over my head?"

"Really?" she replied. "I just thought your friends ate a lot of doughnuts."

"They aren't doing cocaine either," I said sadly.

"If you go gray, it's going to add fifteen years to your age," my sister said. "But you're married, so you have different priorities than I do. I'm single, and the only thing I know how to make for dinner is a cheese board. I need to hang on to my vanity. You have no one left to impress. You're probably going to be okay if you let yourself go."

"But you date bald guys," I said. "You even dated one who was bald and smoked cigars."

"Well, I'm not shallow," she informed me. "But I don't date anyone shorter than five foot eleven. In heels, I can't be the tallest person in the relationship."

If I go gray, I thought to myself, *will people really think I'm fifteen years older than I am?* Maybe that could actually be a benefit if I ever had to date again. Someone who thought I was seventy would be thrilled to find out that my parts were substantially newer and not so prone to cracking and falling apart.

I backed off my decision and scheduled another appointment with my colorist. I laid down another $170 and a slightly smaller tip. Three weeks later, I was down another $170-plus and started taking to spray-painting my scalp brown to cover the road stripe at two weeks. Three weeks after that, I was back in the colorist's chair before I left to do a reading in Seattle the next day.

In Seattle, I was setting up for the reading when I saw a smiling face coming toward me. It was my friend Carolyn, whom I hadn't seen in almost a decade. Hanging around the bars and listening to bands in our twenties, we were often mistaken for one another. We looked somewhat alike, but the thing that made people confuse us was our similar long, curly brown hair. Except now, things had changed.

My hair was still a somewhat real shade of brown, but Carolyn's was magnificent. Now cropped short, it was a glorious silver that looked striking and beautiful. And, most importantly, Carolyn didn't look sixty-five. She looked timelessly gorgeous.

And I was jealous.

"I wish I had gone gray sooner," she told me. "It's such a relief not having to get my roots done every three weeks."

Three weeks later, back to my colorist I went. Before she left to mix the color, I stopped her.

"Let's go all the way," I declared. "Take me back to my roots."

Three hours later, I went home with Orlando Bloom *Lord of the Rings* hair. Stripped of all the dye, my coiffure had a whitish, straw-like look that made me wish I had indeed bought a hijab.

It took two more trips to the salon, as my colorist and I experimented with tints, rinses, and colors. But, eventually, after a couple of weeks of wearing scarves and hats, I walked out of that salon with shining silver hair.

Carolyn was right. I wish I had done it sooner.

I started getting compliments right away. Women my age—and sometimes younger—regularly asked me how I'd done it. I told them all the same thing: Don't wait if you want to go natural. If you don't like it, you can always go back to the chair.

I posted my new real hair on Facebook, and the response I got was quite encouraging. Many women mentioned that they had been toying with the idea but were afraid it would make them look old.

"To whom?" I asked them. "A teenager? The cashier at Safeway? The woman who is our age and tries to look thirty but everyone knows she's our age? Aren't you proud that you know how to use a dial phone? That you lived a whole, full life without a digital device in your pocket? You remember who Gilligan is! You watched Fonzie jump the shark! You remember when coming in second place was *still* awesome. You know how to use a phone book and roll down a window manually. You probably drove a stick shift. As a kid, you played outside all day until dinner. You lived in a time when you could walk your loved ones all the way to the gate in an airport. The guy who sang your favorite song on the radio wasn't also a model. You know what "Where's the beef?" means and remember when everyone ate Hamburger Helper. You watched *Jaws* at the drive-in. We have seen a lot. We survived Aqua Net. We were the last generation of children to ride in a car without seat belts! And there's nothing shameful in saying that.

"Be bold," I encouraged them. "Be gray. You're not a millennial. You're Generation X. Our mothers went shopping and left us in the car in the summer with the windows rolled up and the doors locked, but we *lived*. We are badasses. Own it!"

Laurie Notaro

I reiterate, we are *badasses*. We are the generation who didn't give a shit, remember? We invented punk rock, then grunge. None of the Kardashians belong in our group, not even the mother. That alone makes us the fairest generation of them all. We didn't invent the internet, but we had the first email addresses, and we remember Netscape and Ask Jeeves. We were the last people to make smoking cool. (I quit more than twenty years ago and still miss it.) We "got" *This Is Spinal Tap*, *Raising Arizona*, and *The Big Lebowski*. We know what is funny. We aren't offended easily. And best of all, we're from the '90s, which makes us the coolest generation of the last century. It was the last good time.

So announce it. Let it show. Don't hide your roots under a hair color that doesn't belong to you anymore.

Oh yeah, and one more thing: Barack Obama is now gray and wears it like a halo.

So maybe we're not young. Do you really want to be? There's nothing wrong with being ourselves, and not the following generation, which still has as much to learn as we already know now.

I still rock combat boots with dresses. I still wear whore-red lipstick. I still call everyone "dude."

I'm still me, and now I have the silver hair to prove that I belong to the coolest generation alive, even if we're not doing cocaine and eating powdered doughnuts at brunch after all.

The Day I Became Invisible

After those intense three weeks of bleaching my hair, wearing a lot of hats, and looking like a corn husk doll, I finally achieved the gray hair I had been hoping for.

Those compliments began immediately, and many of them came from strangers, too, but the change also came with a bonus that I didn't expect and didn't know I wanted.

Almost immediately after the transformation was complete, I began to notice something slightly off about my presence, you could say. Cashiers at the supermarket stopped looking at me when I went through their checkout line. I walked into Macy's, and no one tried to bear spray me with perfume. I went to Home Depot to buy tubing, and not one male employee tried to tell me I was buying the wrong kind.

Something was happening—or had happened—that was definitely true, but I couldn't really figure out *what*. People were finally leaving me alone, and I didn't know why.

It wasn't until I was rolling my groceries through the Safeway parking lot that I realized what had happened to me. There, forgotten on the bottom level of my cart, was a $1.69 bag of russet potatoes.

That I had not paid for.

I was shocked, then embarrassed. I stood in the parking lot deliberating if I should go back and pay for them.

Hell no, I decided.

The week before, I'd bought three peaches at the same store for $3.99 a pound, so I'd basically spent ten bucks. It was expensive, but I really wanted peaches, and I had a weak moment. I put them in a paper bag to ripen, and in two days, when they felt perfect, I bit into the most disgusting, inedible peach I had ever had. I threw it away and sliced open the next two with a knife. Mealy, falling apart, and rotten in the middle. I had spent ten dollars on three rotten peaches, and I was pissed.

So I looked at the potatoes that I had just stolen and realized that Safeway owed me four more bags of potatoes for the revolting, overpriced peaches. No, I was not taking them back!

But how had I just walked right out of the store with them?

Oh my God, I realized. *I have a superpower!*

I am invisible.

I am completely invisible.

It suddenly all made sense. Macy's. Home Depot.

No one can see me! I'm like friggin' Harry Potter!

The excitement I felt in that moment was almost unparalleled, only equaling the moments I'd experienced earlier in life when I discovered that I wasn't pregnant.

Still, despite my glee, I couldn't be sure. Was I *really* invisible, or was I simply a skilled potato shoplifter?

The sewer a block away was being dug up, so I decided to run a test. I walked by at least ten construction workers who were on the job.

Nothing happened.

I walked by again, this time slower, with my hair fluffed up and lipstick reapplied.

Silence.

I am totally fucking invisible, I determined.

Okay, it's true that construction workers shouldn't whistle at a gray: that's perverted. But I've also witnessed guys in hard hats whistle at a ravaged lady tweaker scrambling to steal a bike that she could take apart under a bridge. There's always some asshole who thinks it's funny.

Then I went to get frozen yogurt at a self-serve place. I swirled out three different sugar-free flavors high enough to register myself into an IRONMAN Competition and topped my treat with mochi bits and sprinkles. And then I waited for the college student behind the counter to notice me. Leaning

15

against a freezer, she swiped, swiped, swiped, and without look-ing up, she swiped again, then thumb-typed something and laughed.

Awesome, she can't see me! I thought and walked away, dig-ging into the yogurt.

Still, I thought, *I need to strengthen my test results.* Two experiments weren't enough. Under what conditions could I test my theory that would give me a rock-solid answer? Where could I go to confirm undeniably that I was invisible?

So I went to Best Buy. There are always more blue shirts on that sales floor than any other color by a thousand, and there had always been at least five guys on any prior visit who wanted to help me find a lightning cord. Yet on that day, the day I arrived in all of my gray-haired glory, it appeared as if I was in the store by myself. I lingered; I cleared my throat. I wondered aloud in empty aisles if a PC cord would work on my Mac. I stuffed a package of earbuds in my pocket, waited five seconds, and then took them out again.

I could walk out with a laptop, I realized, plus a handful of Post-it Notes.

My hypothesis was proven. I was entirely invisible.

I laughed to myself on the way out, marveling at my new abilities.

I can do anything I want, I sang inside my head. *I'm like a spy now, slipping in and out of realms like a vampire. I'm just like a ghost!*

That was it, I finally understood. I was not really invisible, but I was now the ghost of who I used to be. Someone whom society valued, saw potential in, and considered vibrant and young and worthwhile.

I was the ghost of someone who mattered.

And, I will admit, that initially upset me. I drove home feeling like a shell, like I was worthless and too old to have any importance anymore. Like the best part of my life had passed—the most noteworthy part—and all I had to look forward to was a future in which no one would see me anymore. Then the guy in the car behind me laid on his horn as I paused at a Yield sign to merge with traffic. I looked up, and in the rearview mirror I could see a younger man in a red truck getting very animated because I wasn't moving fast enough for him.

"The sign says 'yield,' not 'forge ahead with total disregard for human life,'" I yelled at the rearview.

When traffic was clear, I made my move and was not surprised when the red truck behind me floored it and tried to pass me but instead ended up next to me at a red light.

He glanced over at me with a disgusted look, thinking I was just an old lady in a beat-up Prius. He looked quite shocked when I rolled the window down and screamed, "Fuck yourself, hillbilly!"

Old lady ghosts aren't supposed to say that. They aren't. But this one does. And even young men with big red trucks don't know how to react when an old punk rock girl throws some shit back at them and it hits them in the face.

I felt so powerful that I wanted to go to Costco and wheel out a freezer on a dolly while waving around an old Safeway receipt, just because I knew I could. It's easy. I'm supposed to be so harmless and weak and afraid that no one pays attention. But those weeks of dye stripping and returning to my natural state created a phenomenon in which the world had literally become mine for the taking.

Now don't get me wrong; I'm not advocating that all mature women start helping themselves to a late-in-life five-finger discount, but if you're going to fail to notice my existence, I'm entitled to a rotisserie chicken every now and then. But what I *do* say is that if you're invisible, if you've made it this far in life, make demands. Guess what you can do now? You can ask for the senior discount at movie theaters, which is pretty much the same as a child's admission price, and no one will question you. I also sneak drinks, candy, *and* popcorn in. No one is going to say anything to me. And if they do, I will say that on most days I eat cat food on a fixed budget, so piss off. I order kids' meals at restaurants, and the server just nods without question. Old lady. Little appetite, if she even lives through the meal.

My friend Sara posted on Facebook that her air conditioner died on a 123-degree day in Phoenix. As the repair guy was leaving, he said to her, "You're nice. I'm going to give you the senior discount." She was shocked and didn't know what to say. *Nice* is not the first word I would use to describe Sara. For background, I've seen her, at five foot two, bounce guys ten times her size out of the bar she managed. I've seen her cut off mean drunks and make bullies cry. I also made her wear velvet when she was one of my bridesmaids. Thousands of people in the greater Phoenix area are terrified of Sara, and if you live in Arizona, you already know who I'm talking about. But Sara as an old lady was not sitting well with her, and she had turned to Facebook to complain.

"How much did you save?" I asked her in the comments section.

"Five hundred dollars," she replied.

"Then who gives a shit what they call it?" I posted. "You got a five-hundred-dollar discount. Now take that money, go see a six-dollar movie, and eat dinner at a restaurant for three dollars and get a free apple juice. You just won a five-hundred-dollar lottery ticket. I just stole potatoes from Safeway. Your A/C score was legendary!"

"I don't think I'll ever feel like a senior," she responded. "At least not in my heart."

But on that Facebook thread, all the middle-aged ghosts came out.

"Ten percent off at Kroger for groceries the first Wednesday of the month!" one of our friends posted.

"Way ahead of you. AARP discounts rock," said our friend Keith, a singer in a punk band.

"You're just a senior at Rock and Roll High School," someone else posted.

"Own it," said our friend Jim, who recently retired and now writes seventeen-page letters to his cable company in protest of price increases. "I take advantage of every senior discount I can get."

Then, in the best post ever, Sara put two granny-face emojis in her reply, followed by, "Gen X, motherfuckers!!"

And every single person on that thread saw it.

What's Happening?: A User's Manual for Your New Old Body

Hello, you. Or what used to be you, I should say. Because at a certain point in life, things start getting a little weird.

I know you're facing a scary time. Your body is changing, odd things are happening, and many times it's difficult to comprehend what is falling, failing, or has stopped working altogether. This manual for your disintegrating body will hopefully answer some questions you've had for a while—How do I get up off the floor? What was that popping noise? Should I call my doctor or my life insurance agent first? Do I *have* to shop at Chico's now? I stopped smoking thirty years ago. When is it safe to start again?—and others that will prepare you for what is to come. Because wherever you are on the journey of aging, tomorrow is going to be both worse and better.

After Facebook outed all of us, I assembled an expert team of MAWs (middle-aged women) to weigh in and offer expert advice. The more advice we shared with one another, the more we were able to concentrate on the fun parts of aging, like heckling teenagers without them seeing it coming. Lucky you, reader, that you get to reap the benefit of our collective experience and relegate more of your time to enjoying these golden years. Gird your loins! Remember that there are upsides, and let's get started!

1. INVEST IN COPIOUS AMOUNTS OF BODY POWDER.

One morning, somewhere in the middle of my false menopausal transition, I woke up and my inner thighs were stuck together like two raw chicken breasts. Prying them apart took a good deal of effort and involved a lot of whimpering. I nearly required skin grafts to repair the resulting damage. Your body is slowly melting, and it will continue to do so until the day you die. It is losing its ability to remain upright, and, like plastic wrap, will cling to the closest object. But it's fine. Like raw chicken, you must simply dredge yourself in flour. All areas of contact will need a hearty dusting twice daily—especially after showering. Dust that smile of flesh that has magically appeared right above your bald monkey. Dust your underboobs, your inner thighs, and your plumber's crack, if you're feeling flashy. These are all danger areas for rash development and ingrown hairs. The scent of an Italian deli may sometimes waft out of said areas.

Expert Tip: "You're going to need baby powder more than any baby."—Jennifer Rodger, MAW

2. WHAT IS ACID REFLUX?

My husband claims to have acid reflux. My husband is a liar.

"No, I have it," he protests. "After I eat a tomato, it burns in my chest until I eat a TUMS."

That, my friends, is not acid reflux. That is the embryo of acid reflux whose heartbeat isn't even detectable yet.

My first introduction to acid reflux was while I was on a book tour with Jen Lancaster and Quinn Cummings. After a reading in Atlanta, we had a late dinner at Gladys Knight's Chicken & Waffles restaurant. Roughly three hours later, I woke with a flamethrower being shot up from my chest into my throat. Gagging, coughing, and in excruciating pain—you know, the kind that raw stomach acid causes—I decided to drink water (wrong), eat a cracker (wrong), and then search through my luggage as I both wheezed and cried. I found some old Pepto Bismol tablets that had been reduced to dust.

When stomach acid explodes in your throat, it actually burns it, and eating anything is akin to swallowing broken glass. I managed to eat every single tablet that I found, which was six, and then I couldn't talk for two days. I had to depend on Quinn to order milk for me at every opportunity.

When I returned to Eugene, Oregon, I immediately sought out my doctor and explained what happened. He nodded and confirmed it was acid reflux. His solution was a bit less than stellar, as he told me to go to Home Depot, get some two-by-fours, and use them to elevate the head of my bed.

"Is there anything else I can do?" I asked, hoping for a quick fix.

"Don't eat fried food or anything acidic," he responded.

"That is insanity," I replied. "How many two-by-fours?"

A little burning like my husband feels upon ingesting a tomato is not acid reflux. That is agita. Acid reflux tries to eat you alive.

Keep several bottles of Pepto on hand; honey will also help, as will Mrs. Butterworth's. The best thing for coating your throat, believe it or not, is milk chocolate. And good Lord above, do not try to eat a Triscuit. I doubt you'll live.

Expert Tip: "You must ALWAYS have TUMS on hand. Not only will you need them (and there's nothing worse than needing a TUMS and not having one), but you will be able to help your coworker/friend/neighbor out when they are in dire need. You can make someone's day."—Sarah Joyce Baird, MAW

3. WHY IS MY ASS WHERE MY BELLY USED TO BE?

After age forty, when you are sleeping, your ass moves, fat cell by fat cell, traveling over treacherous terrain, like penguins, and claims its new territory in your abdomen. This happens, night after night, like family members you have left back in New Jersey. They will come, shifting the mass from stern to bow. The more deflated and flappy your ass gets, the more extended that belly becomes, until you resemble an exhausted party balloon from behind and a snowman from the front.

Expert Tip: "Should have kept doing sit-ups and squats . . . It's not pretty to harrumph off the couch. You spill your ice cream."—Lori Frijole, MAW

4. CAN BENDING OVER KILL ME?

Yes, it can. Bid goodbye to anything that is below waist height. It's not worth the agony. One night, my husband was bending over trying to find the right piece of Tupperware in the bottom cabinet when I asked him if he had seen the Parmesan cheese.

"I could answer your question," he could barely spit out, "or I could focus on staying alive."

Bending over is a thing of the past. Whatever I toss in the bottom two drawers of the fridge will evolve into a wonderful compost soup because I cannot collect the courage required to lean into the refrigerator and get it back out. Even if it's 120 degrees outside and all I want is something cool and crunchy, the lettuce will liquefy because I cannot bear the thought of either listening to my knees crackle like Cap'n Crunch or having them sway and buckle until my kneecap pops off and becomes an ankle cap. I cannot bear that lowering myself from the waist down will force one fat roll to collide with another like Earth's tectonic plates, and the subduction energy that results will bring me faster to unconsciousness than sniffing glue.

Expert Tip: "Stop putting things in lower cabinets, because you won't be able to get them out. Ever."—Kim Collins, MAW

5. SNEAKER FARTS.

I take no pleasure in reporting that—if it hasn't already happened—it is possible to fart without effort. You'll be doing absolutely nothing, and it'll slip out like air from a ragged old tire. If you've ever seen your dog do it, you will have a very similar reaction. Shock. Horror. Disgust. But look—how many fifty-year-old rubber bands still do the job? There's only so much stretch and pull one little muscle can take before it needs to take a nap, and a sneaker fart gets through.

But wait! There's more! Sneaker farts often take advantage of movement, sneezes, and coughs to free themselves from their dark human prison. I know I wouldn't want to be trapped in my own ass, but a jailbreak is never appreciated. I've heard that this happens a lot in yoga classes, though I wouldn't know because I don't believe in that bullshit. But say you're at a dinner party and a drumroll just launched from your rectum. My suggestion is, in the next second, declare you have been taking lessons to become a fart ventriloquist and that was one of your finest creations. Honestly, I would probably just fish out a dirty Valium from the bottom of my purse, take it, and go home.

Expert Tip: "The surprise farts are some bullshit, I tell you what. I leaned over at my therapy appointment last week and blasted a duck quack out of my ass that I had no idea was sitting there ready to go."—Princess Dana McFierciepants, MAW

6. WHAT'S THE DEAL WITH MY EYEBROWS?

Starting this very minute, leave them alone. I'm serious. Pluck only the most egregious of hairs; get eyebrow scissors and trim them instead. This is literally the only piece of advice my mother had to offer about getting old. A few years ago, during a visit with my parents, I met my mother in the hallway immediately after she woke up and before she was able to put on her makeup. I looked at her, not able to place why, exactly, she looked like the Thompson Twins.

Then I gasped. "Where are your eyebrows?!"

She frowned. "In my bathroom cabinet, where they've been since 1985."

"You have fake eyebrows?" I asked, still shocked.

"Don't be an idiot," she snapped. "What, do you think they come like fake eyelashes? I draw them on. In fact, they are the only thing I can draw."

She headed off to the bathroom but then stopped and turned.

"You'd better not put this in a book," she warned. "Because it's going to happen to you too. You get to a certain point, and you're as hairless as a newborn baby."

I have taken that advice as if it were a stone tablet I found next to a burning bush.

Though men's eyebrows continue to grow full and sturdy enough to make Cher wigs from, many women's eyebrows suffer the opposite fate. They grow thinner and thinner until, one day, your own daughter can barely recognize you without the aid of Maybelline.

Expert Tip: "DO NOT OVERPLUCK YOUR F-N EYEBROWS FOR THE LOVE OF JESUS!!"—Kerry Dill-Genova, MAW

7. Hey. The back of my head looks like my dad's.

If you don't think you are thinning, get a hand mirror and take a gander at the back of your head. If you're like me, you resemble a monk back there, and I recommend avoiding purchasing any brown linen dresses, lest you want to hear someone's confession. Yes, your hair is probably thinning. It doesn't happen to everyone (my friend Jamie never met a drain she couldn't choke to death with one good brushing), but the good news is that technology has *finally* caught up with the balding woman.

Remember the root spray color I used to extend trips to the colorist? Guess what can disguise thin spots too? The same thing! Spray hair! I know we all laughed at the Ronco guy in the '80s who marketed hair in a can, but he was onto something. You just have to be careful not to go all Rudy Giuliani and use so much that it drools down your face like an oil rig is hovering above you.

My sister also gave me a pair of clip-in hair extensions, and between these and the spray hair, I can return to the head of hair I had twenty years ago. The best part: I don't have to wash it as often, and when I do, I very much enjoy hanging the extensions from the shower curtain rod as if they were scalps and hoping that the hobo in the alley with binoculars sees them.

It is also worth noting that hair will migrate from private to public regions, such as your chin and neck. The hairs colonize, and as soon as one successfully grows to a certain length without being detected, it sends vibrations to invite others, like ants. The hairs on your chinny chin chin can arrive as early as your teens, but if you're lucky enough to largely avoid that, they will definitely pop up by the time you're in your forties. To conquer these foes (because they are not just gray hairs by this time—they are translucent, like creatures from the deepest depths of the ocean), you need a dependable pair of tweezers (forget Revlon; think something that surgeons use to remove shrapnel) and one of the following: a good husband with at least +4.00 readers, a secluded and sunny parking spot, and a clean rearview mirror, or someone who owes you a lot of money.

My chin and neck hairs are almost invisible, and I have hunted some for more than seven days in a row. I try to capture them in a variety of lighting and timing scenarios: upstairs bathroom, downstairs bathroom, work bathroom, spreading my skin tight with one hand while I go in for the kill with the other, under the flashlight from my iPhone, after a hot shower, and first thing in the morning, when they think I'm still asleep and are still busy growing and not camouflaging themselves like puffer fish.

Chin hairs are elusive, sneaky organisms. They are simply put there so that you cannot think about anything else but the victory yank when you finally have them by the root and out of your body. I personally believe that chin hairs are most likely responsible for several plane crashes, oil spills, detonated bombs, and many, many unplanned babies.

I highly recommend inspecting the hair, once it's in the grip of the tweezers at last. I have to see my enemy, the cause of so much anxiety, and I have to curse it as I finally release it and let it fall into the trash can. Sometimes I point and swear at it. Call it names. Tell it who the boss *really* is.

Expert Tip: "I got a wig in the mail by mistake. It worked. Daddy loved it. I wore it once."—My mother, who wishes to remain anonymous

8. WHAT SHOULD I DO WHEN I FEEL A SHARP, UNEXPLAINABLE PAIN ANYWHERE IN MY BODY?

Call your State Farm agent and up your life insurance by a lot. *Then* call a doctor's office.

I am not kidding.

Expert Tip: "Pray to God. I would never go to a doctor."—My mother, who wishes to remain anonymous

9. SHOULD I GO FOR A FULL-BODY SKIN SCAN?

Yes. If you grew up someplace where the sun shines for at least a day out of the year, yes. It is almost as horrible an experience as a colonoscopy, and only better because poop generally isn't involved. However, you still have to get naked, lie on a table, and have a stranger examine every inch of you as if they are trying to pick out the best doughnut. When a lot of people my age were teenagers, the summer meant three things: Fleetwood Mac on the boom box, a lounge chair, and an enormous bottle of baby oil.

Now that all distills to one thing: skin cancer.

Because I grew up in Phoenix, my dermatologist insisted that I succumb to a full-body scan. I was having a mole removed at the time.

"I can't," I tried to explain. "I was raised Catholic."

She didn't understand, and for those of you who don't either, let me try to explain. If you're Catholic and someone to whom you aren't married sees you even close to being naked, you've basically just had dirty, nasty sex with them. You've just been coated with Whore, and it stays that way your entire life. You can't ever get it off. When I was five, I refused to watch *Mr. Peabody & Sherman* cartoons because I was convinced that "body" was a filthy word and that I would go to hell for hearing it. Any other little baby Catholics feel that way?

So imagine me fifteen minutes after my doctor insisted that I allow the full inspection. I have never been so sober and so naked in my entire life. I thought this kind of scrutiny was reserved for corpses that died under mysterious circumstances. But there I was, having my own live autopsy being performed under million-watt lights.

"Are you the Laurie Notaro that writes the books?" the doctor paused to ask. The same thing happens to me every single time my credit card gets declined or I'm at a doctor's office for private reasons.

Every. Single. Time.

"No," I said, my eyes squeezed so tight it was like I was trying to wring every bit of Mr. Peabody shame out of me. "I hate her."

"For growing up in Arizona, you barely have any sun damage," she exclaimed, and at that I finally exhaled.

"In 1981, punk rock happened, and we all went inside," I informed her.

So, again, the answer is that you absolutely need it. Even if you and I were hanging out in a house on Third Avenue and Edgemont that had all of the windows blocked out with tinfoil, get your full-body scan done if you haven't already had an autopsy.

Expert Tip: "You should get a full-body scan, absolutely. It might be the only action you get in a while. Just like when I get a massage, ask for a male and try to find out his name. You want a Justin, Ryan, or Brian."—Lisa Notaro

10. How do I get rid of saggy, crepey skin?

That's something you needed to think about in your twenties. You should have been at hospital cafeterias spouse-shopping for plastic surgery residents, not at bars where you smuggled in your own alcohol.

I'm sorry. That ship has sailed away with sagging, crepey sails.

Expert Tip: "Well, you get this stuff called Crepe and start rubbing it into your skin when you're eight. But it doesn't matter because it really doesn't work. I do it for peace of mind."—My mother, who wishes to remain anonymous

11. How should I pack for trips now that I'm a senior citizen?

It absolutely doesn't matter. No need to waste your time! No one is looking at you. Collect six of your favorite ointments and some powder and you're done.

Expert Tip: "Why are you going anywhere? You're too old to walk around. Watch it on TV. You don't have to pack nothing."— My mother, who wishes to remain anonymous

12. Why are my ankles swollen?

Salt intake, circulation issues, hot weather, your name is Hillary Clinton, you just got off a plane that crossed over Texas, or someone put a curse on you. Who knows. All I know is that if I'm traveling anywhere, by the time I land, my ankles will look like a python who snuck out of its cage at a pet store and paid a visit to a colony of rats. Bring water pills with you, and wear compression socks (they look just like regular socks). For most people, swollen ankles are seasonal, really only affecting them at a time of the year when people will actually see their ankles.

The best news is that you probably still have your Docs, and this is indeed the very best time to wear them.

Expert Tip: "Your ankles are swollen from carrying the weight of the patriarchy all of these years."—Danika Hill, MAW

13. THERE IS A DESERT WHERE A RAIN FOREST USED TO BE. I DON'T KNOW WHAT TO DO.

Sister. Sister. I know. It's like someone stuck a Shop-Vac hose up there and left it on for a month. I get it.

As my friend Angela puts it, it's "like an open clam in the sun on the boardwalk."

This is my *best* advice: There are products that can help. If you buy them on Amazon, it will forever be in your order history, and one day, the police will probably see it and ask you about it if you are a homicide suspect. If you talk about it in your house, Siri will tell her friends, and it will start popping up in ads on Facebook and Instagram. If you buy it at Safeway with cash, you're going to have to stand there while the teenaged cashier studies it like it was a new planet he discovered, saying, "Huh. I've never seen this before. What's it for?"

If that happens, I want you to say, "Call your mother on your next break and ask her what vaginal dryness is. *And then never ask that question to anyone ever again.*"

You get to decide which humiliation suits you best.

Once you have the product, you need to put it in a very special place. And I mean a very special place (no, not there, not yet) so that, in the dark, you will know exactly how to find it when you need it. Do not put it in a drawer with tubes of toothpaste, arthritis cream, and Tinactin. Do not buy something—any product—that comes in a container that is in the least bit similar to a Vicks or IcyHot jar.

Put a bell or a night light on it if you have to. Because if you do not follow my advice, vaginal dryness will no longer be your most pressing problem, and your dried-up old clam will probably catch fire.

14. I am no longer housebroken. Help!

I warned everyone about this in one of my earlier books: I try not to pee too often because those parts wear out, and they don't have replacement parts for them yet. That was twenty years ago, and still, I'm afraid that no one considers lady leaks an issue that needs solving. The best anyone can do is make mini pads that we have to wear until our dying day because, basically, after a certain age, you can pee anytime. You can pee during a sneeze, a cough, or a nice laugh. You can pee simply while you're getting up or sitting down. There is no warning: it just . . . trickles. For instance, my friend Amy took me for a ride in her fresh-off-the-lot new car, and halfway to our destination, I felt it—all warm all over my bottom. To be honest, it actually felt rather nice. I had no idea what my next move was going to be, and as she found a parking spot at Mrs. White's Soul Food, I was on the verge of tears when she said, "How do you like those seat warmers?"

"Holy shit, I thought I just pissed my pants!" I screamed out of relief. "But it felt so good!"

That had a happy ending, but the possibility is always there, and we live on with that fear. But unlike all the girl-power period marketing, there's no campaign to make us feel comfortable talking about it. I've never gone into my coworker's office and said, "Paula, do you have a puppy pad I can borrow in case I urinate all over myself like a drunk in the staff meeting? I was running a little late this morning and forgot my training pants."

Funny thing is, I never pee the bed at night, not even a little. My body is still in tune enough to wake me up when I have to go, and then, as a thank-you for the alarm bell, I get to spend the rest of the night trying to go back to sleep and drinking NyQuil out of the bottle.

Expert tip: "We now need wee-wee pads and have to change them as if we will have our periods 24-7 for the rest of our damn lives. I mean, menopause was supposed to have some benefits. I mention wee-wee pads because with every flipping cough, sneeze, and laugh, we get a gush of urine. Yes, I said gush. Dribbles were in our forties."—Tina Willet Craig, MAW

15. How do I know I am middle-aged?

The first time you grunt, gasp, or moan while attempting to get up off anything is the Bat-Signal that you are middle-aged.

And the first time that you see something advertised and really want it, but then you immediately think about ways you could get hurt using it. I just saw a pair of aqua-blue old-school roller skates for sale at Saks on my Instagram feed. And I want them. I want them badly. I even went through the checkout process to see how much shipping would be. And it was free. Damn it. But even though they were $139, and I am *happy* to pay that, I can't roller skate in my parents' carport, or up and down the street. I'd look like an asshole. I mean, capitalize the *K* in Krazy Lady for that one. But the most alarming aspect is how much those roller skates would actually cost me in medical bills, hospitalization fees, and time lost from work. Not to mention the lie mountain I would have to build to create a narrative about how I broke my hip and arm and needed a skin graft on my chin, all from one incident that didn't involve a large piece of machinery and a cheese grater.

Expert Tip: "Can you count? Are you stupid? You hit fifty. You're middle-aged."—My mother, who wishes to remain anonymous

16. MY BOOBS ARE STRETCHING LIKE SALTWATER TAFFY. WHY?

Well, for a lot of reasons. Maybe you were a hippie as a youngster and danced a lot at Phish concerts. Babies. Genetics. All of the women in my immediate family—me, my two sisters, and my mother—always expect a second, third, or fourth round of poking and prodding after our mammograms. "Dense breast tissue," I warn my doctor, and after every mammogram, MRI, core punch biopsy—Ever had that? It's awesome. It's like a corn-hole game but with your boob and a hole puncher—or surgery, I'll finally get the results that tell me "dense breast tissue."

But mainly, it's gravity. What allows you to walk upright on this earth also makes you sag, just like what makes you happy and fun at parties will make you try to buy a liver on eBay in a couple of decades.

What can you do? The obvious. Go Real Housewife and get those tatas propped up, or invent a pulley system. The most important thing you do, however, is go right back to tip #1: powder. Because it's not bad enough that your nipples can graze your thighs just by sitting down, they can also cook up quite a stink with boob sweat. Powder them gently, on top and underneath, with the most glorious of scents. If they're going to look like sweet potatoes, they might as well smell like roses.

Expert Tip: "I wish someone had told me that my 34Bs would become 36 Longs."—Kirby Dunton Carespodi, MAW

17. WHY CAN'T I LOSE WEIGHT AFTER FIFTY?

Because you are lazy. Because you are addicted to food. Because you didn't take care of yourself when you were younger. Because you'd rather watch TV than go to the gym. Because you love cake.

Because, because, because.

At least, that's what a bad doctor will tell you, and then he will send his nurse in to introduce you to MyFitnessPal, even though you weren't at the doctor's office for a weight-related issue to begin with. You never even brought your weight up.

I'm not a doctor, but I am a friend. And almost all of my friends have weight issues, except for the ones who have anxiety so badly that they barely eat. I have gone on long, extended vacations with friends, spending almost twenty-four hours a day with them. And I will tell you that not one time have I woken up in the middle of the night to listen to my friend scarf down a dozen bagels or eat an entire cake that they have hidden, slice by slice, in their shoes.

My friends are not overeaters. They don't have waffles and fried chicken at every meal. So I've come to the conclusion that obesity is caused by something we simply don't understand yet, and the reason why people are still obese is that no one really cares that much to figure it out. What makes me an expert? I'm obese, and I know what I eat, and I know what I have to do to lose weight, and I also know it's not sustainable.

I have been singing this song for thirty years.

I have watched my friends suffer through liquid diets, doctor-prescribed diets with food that shakes out of envelopes, and diets that eliminate every healthy food and substitute a ball of cheese for an apple.

Obesity is an industry. It makes people billions of dollars because us chubs are so very desperate to become un-chubs. We can't lose weight after fifty because our metabolism slows down, and we don't know how to fix that.

Yet. I bet it's going to take a chunky woman with a big brain, swollen ankles, and a well-funded lab to figure out why losing weight after fifty is like scaling a glacier in flip-flops.

And I will totally volunteer to be a test subject.

Expert Tip: "The day will come when you fervently wish that you are only as fat as you were the FIRST time you thought you were fat."—Michelle Loyet, MAW, whom I've been on vacation with numerous times

18. Why can't I remember anything anymore?

In my book, you really only have to remember two things: to brush your teeth and where your insurance card is.

Everything else is a bonus. Don't stress about this part of aging. Look at it the right way, and it's a blessing.

Frankly, there is just too much information out there, and they keep sending more shit my way. I'm on eight different platforms at work, and there are four types of ways people can communicate with me that don't include texts, iPhones, office phones, real mail, or a note folded up like a football. I just got an alert that told me 127 of my passwords have been compromised and I should change them all. Now.

How do I have 127 passwords? If I took the time that I used just to create them, I could have gotten a better college degree or gone to Europe.

And I'm not memorizing new passwords. No way. God knows what I'd lose in the exchange. How to get home? What I'm allergic to? My medical history? The memory of being labeled the whore of high school journalism camp because I snuck my friend's vodka bottle in my purse on the way to the roller-skating event? It was the first time I ever became NOTORIOUS, and my seventeen-year-old newspaper editor shook her finger at me and told me she was "ashamed." I want to remember that occasion, in case I ever meet her again. Preferably in a parking lot.

There's all kinds of stuff that I don't remember from only days ago. One time, I had to collect a twenty-four-hour urine sample for my doctor, and I seriously don't remember why. She told me why; I just let that memory fly away like a moth. Imagine my surprise at the lab when they brought out a red gas can and what looked like a white plastic nun's wimple. The lab tech put both items in a plain plastic bag for me, and I walked out of the hospital swinging it like it was a bag of candy. Only when I got into the car did I see the other side, printed in huge letters:

24-Hour Urine Sample

(Biohazard symbol in red and black)

When I got home, my husband laughed until he found out that I needed to keep it in the fridge next to his almond milk.

"Why are you doing this?" he asked.

"I don't know," I replied.

"I mean, what's the purpose of it?" he rephrased.

I shrugged. "No idea."

"But why is your doctor making you do this?" he tried again.

"Beats me," I explained. "She told me, but my memory is like an overstuffed Chinese commuter train. You can fight your way in, but, ultimately, something is going to fall out and get left on the tracks. Looks like the pee jug fell out."

I'm hoping I'll eventually find out, because I noticed that the almond milk carton was in the recycling, and all other food within a six-inch circumference of the jug was in the sink, ready to meet the InSinkErator.

My point is: the problem is not that we are losing our memory. It's that we are at capacity, and if new stuff wants to come in, we have to start throwing old stuff overboard. I deleted seventh and eighth grade just to remember the names of my coworkers once I started my new job. Frankly, I can't handle any new stuff. I really don't even want new stuff. I held out on getting a smart TV because I couldn't bear the thought of trying to figure out how to work it, and not only work it, but *remember* how to work it, and that, my friends, was the right thing to do. Stick with things you understand when your husband majored in poetry and not engineering. When I finally broke down and got a smart TV, there was a whole entire galaxy of options—apps, channels, subscriptions, the Roku remote, the regular remotes, and then something called "casting." I heard about a show called *Escape to the Chateau* and became convinced I couldn't live without it, but I couldn't get the app to work on the smart TV, because I think the Costco guy didn't sell me a smart TV, but one that just had a GED. I tried screen mirroring; getting a new Roku; using an old Apple TV box that had literally been sitting in a drawer, unopened, since 2012; buying a new FireWire cable; and trying an unmarked cable that looked like it might work. Finally, I put an ad on Facebook:

WANTED: Teenager to help two old people figure out how to cast Escape to the Chateau *from their phones to their TV. We do not know what kind of TV it is. We think we have iPhones. We made a mistake by not having children eighteen years ago, and we are willing to pay the going rate to make up for that now. Nephew could not help us because he was helping his grandmother put an attachment on an email and was visibly upset when we FaceTimed him.*

Eventually, after we didn't get any bites, I even offered to fly my nephew from Phoenix to Oregon just so we could figure it out.

"I told you during the last visit I was there that if you asked me one more time to help pluck your chin hairs, I wasn't coming back," he told me. "You held that tweezer to me like it was a knife, Aunt Laurie."

And then, one day, the TV just worked. Don't ask me how. I don't remember, and I'm glad I don't because I don't know who or what I made a pact with so I could watch another middle-aged couple buy a castle and fix it up.

In the end, it was worth it; it's a great show, but I am dying with this TV. I just can't go through it again. And, for the record, this is not like trying to teach Nana how to work a VCR. It is not. There are no passwords on a VCR, no usernames you have to type in one by one, then @gmail.com. If I could do it all over again, in 2000, I would have scored the email address 1@gmail.com. Who thought idiotgirlsruletheworld@gmail.com would cause so many fights with my husband or that it would eventually give us both repetitive motion injuries? *Who has 1@gmail.com, and how much do you want for it?*

19. WHY DOES MY BODY HURT IN A DIFFERENT PLACE EVERY DAY, AND WHAT CAN I DO ABOUT IT?

Last week, my eye hurt so much that I thought it was going to pop out of my head and hit the wall. I swore that, in the morning, I would get the next available doctor's appointment, which wasn't for eight months and would probably be the day after my husband pushed me on rollers into an oven in a cardboard box after I died from eye cancer.

The following day, the tendons that keep my kneecap in place felt like Twizzlers, and I feared that I was going to be trapped upstairs forever, dependent on my husband to bring me food when he remembered that I was up there. (He would not be willing to trade seventh or eighth grade for that nugget of information.)

The day after that, I got up out of a chair and wrenched my thigh muscle so badly that I had to dip into my emergency-only painkillers from when I got impaled.

The day after that, the second toe on my left foot ached for hours, as if I had broken it.

The day after that, I ate a Triscuit, and one of my molars collapsed, as if the Taliban had mistaken it for a holy relic and blown it up.

There is so much responsibility in getting older. There are so many pills to take for sore eyes, dry eyes, dry mouth, rubber-band knees, achy toes, low blood pressure, high blood pressure.

What I do know is that when I was five, I got a doll named Betsy. She was made out of thick pink plastic. She moved with me all the way into adulthood, and I brought her to Oregon with me. Last week, I was digging through some boxes in the basement, and I found her. Her hair was matted, her skin jaundice yellow, but there she was, lying peacefully in a cardboard box for all this time. In a moment of sentimentality, I reached out and picked her up, only to have her completely disintegrate in my hands. She actually splintered into shards of ocher plastic and clattered to the floor in a tumble of what looked like picnic knives.

So this leads me to consider that: (1) Betsy was made from something that cannot properly disintegrate and is completely artificial, and (2) she was younger than me, so I should be happy that I'm not on the basement floor in a pile of bone shards. In fact, I do believe that if I fell into a deep enough sleep with a space heater on me, I would begin to decompose and melt into a big enough puddle that the sheriff's department would have to stuff towels under my front door to keep me from leaking out onto the porch. It has happened to someone. *It has.*

Of course, there are some things you can do to prevent age-related mystery pain. I try to do some warm-up exercises while still in bed. I rotate my ankles to make sure that they're still working. I stretch out my back so that I don't knock a disk out while standing up. I move my shoulders around like a strip-per (sorry, I meant sex-work-related "dancer"). Of course, the biggest challenge is not wetting myself by making any sudden movements.

The other thing to do is load up on extra-strength Tylenol and hope you don't outlive your liver. Or take yoga classes and fart in front of strangers.

In the end, I have finally come to this conclusion: at my age, if it hurts on both sides equally, it's completely normal.

Expert Tip: "No matter how old and achy I am, I can still haul ass outta bed when the dog starts making vomit noises."—Connie Sherretts, MAW

20. Once I get down on the floor, I can't get back up again. Help!

The main thing to remember here is, *never* lower yourself to the ground level unless you have a large piece of furniture within arm's reach or someone in your family owns an excavator with a chain and a hook. If you have foolishly plopped yourself on the floor without either, here are some techniques to try.

Gorilla Pose:
From a cross-legged position, uncross your legs and bring them into a fetal position. Then clench your hands so that the knuckles are facedown and plant them on the ground, like an ape. If you

have your palms flattened on the floor, expect electric bolts of pain to shoot up through your arms due to carpal tunnel syndrome.

Once you have your hands in place, move to all fours. You are now in Gorilla Pose.

Hoist:
Assume Gorilla Pose. Bring one leg up, using your gorilla hands to provide support, and place one foot on the floor, then the other. From there, you may be able to stand upright if you haven't popped a disk or used an atrophied muscle that hasn't been activated in twenty years.

Rollin', Rollin', Rollin':
From a sitting pose, stretch your legs in front of you, and recline slowly. Once you are parallel to the floor, cross your arms in front of your chest, heave your body weight to the left or right—one, two, three times for propulsion—and roll until you bump into something large and, preferably, twice your body weight.

Once you have reached your target, assume Gorilla Pose, then grab the item and lift yourself to safety.

Crab Crawl:
Determine a target. From a cross-legged position, stretch your legs in front of you, and then bend until the bottom of your feet make contact with the floor. Relax your arms to your sides,

then place your palms on the floor. Alternate feet and arm movements until you achieve a steady scurrying movement and arrive at your destination. Assume Gorilla Pose, and rise.

Impulse Shopping:
Sometimes, all the Gorilla Poses and Hoists in the world aren't enough. As a MAW, the safest defense is to order something online at least every other day to ensure that a rescue is imminent, should the other techniques fail. When that happens, allow yourself to collapse, and save your strength for screaming when the mail carrier arrives.

Expert Tip: "I taught you to crawl to the closest chair and bring yourself up. Do you need me to write you a note to keep up your sleeve?"—My mother, who wishes to remain anonymous

21. WHAT WAS THAT POPPING NOISE COMING FROM INSIDE MY BODY?

I have no idea, but I'm pretty sure it's the equivalent of your check-engine light coming on. My knees make the sound of Cap'n Crunch, my guts begin a gurgling symphony after I take a bite of anything, and then there's the popping.

I'm sure the popping is a sign that my inner scaffolding of tendons and hamstrings is either collapsing because the point of contact has accumulated too much dog hair to still stick like a Post-it Note, or it is surrendering to forces unknown. I am positive that there is only one ligament left holding the whole show together, and that with one attempt to land on a toilet seat lower than it appears, I could be reduced to what looks like a giant mound of butter wearing a wig.

But it's really the cracking that I'm afraid of. I once turned my head two inches and heard that awful sound—and froze for as long as I could stand it, sure that I had just broken my own neck. Once I unfroze, I believed that my head would fall forward, and I would be strangled by my own neck rolls.

If my car made the sounds that my body does, I'd grudgingly drive it to the nearest dealership and would even consider trading it in for a Fiat. I mean, I'm certain that some parts have been recalled, and I threw the notices away, thinking they were junk mail, and now I have no legal recourse. If you know the lawyer who is handling the class-action suit for disintegrating knee cartilage, please email me their number.

However, I've defied the odds this far, and if I move as little as possible, I'm hoping to keep most things in their rightful place.

Expert Tip: "At this point in my life, I have trouble telling whether someone in my house is making microwave popcorn or if it's my knees going up the stairs."—Kimberly Veilleux, MAW

22. WHY IS MY SKIN SO DRY AND . . . BUMPY?

As I have aged, I have developed the complexion of an orange peel. Lotion doesn't help. Exfoliating scrubs don't help. Oil doesn't help. I flake like a croissant, and there are some areas of my skin that are so thin I can read through them, like a laminated pastry in human form. I never had great skin anyway, so there wasn't much to lose, but now I look at every dot, bump, and follicle and wonder about "margins."

If you want to know anything about skin cancer, don't go to a dermatologist. (I mean, do get the full-body check, but other than that, don't go straight to the dermatologist.) Just find a girl who grew up in Arizona, used to baste her body in oil like it was duck confit, and lay in the sun for eight hours a day with a tinfoil-wrapped piece of cardboard to help the cancer along. They'll tell you exactly what it is and possibly save you a co-pay. My friend Amy can look at a suspect freckle and deliver a basal, squamous, melanoma, or Merkel cell carcinoma diagnosis in two seconds flat. Everyone in Arizona has skin cancer. It's so common that it should really appear on the license plate instead of a cactus. Both of my parents had skin cancer in the exact same spot—right below the bridge of the nose. The scars are semicircular, and they match, making me wonder if we now have a new family crest that resembles the hammer and sickle on the Soviet flag.

So, honestly, I don't even know why my own skin is so dry and bumpy, but I do know that I can see a rotisserie chicken relate all too well.

Expert Tip: "Because as you get older, moisture leaks through everywhere. Your body starts to mummify before you die. It's just getting you ready for death."—My mother, who prefers to remain anonymous

23. Do I *have* to shop at Chico's now?

Years ago, when I was on a book tour, I realized that traveling to thirty different cities in thirty-two days meant that I needed to pack light. The common denominator in most of my outfits was cowboy boots and a vintage dress. So that's what I brought and managed to squeeze into one carry-on: four vintage dresses, cowboy boots that I wore constantly, and thirty-one pairs of underwear.

The day after my stop in Ann Arbor, I was talking to my publicist, who'd called to ask me what I had been wearing. Apparently, my escort in Ann Arbor had told her that she'd been thrilled to see me in costume as my character Idiot Girl.

But it wasn't a costume, I told the publicist. It was my Tuesday/Friday outfit, a black-and-silver 1950s patio dress from Tucson that was in perfect condition.

I still have that dress and the cowboy boots, and I expect to still be wearing them until I die. I'm not going to dress my age;

Laurie Notaro

I'm going to dress as me. Although I will admit that I have a bigger collection of flats than I ever had before, I'm most comfortable in the clothes that are mine. And if that means that a woman from Ann Arbor thinks I'm dressing up as a character in a book in which the character is me, she is damn well right.

So if you like Chico's clothes, wear Chico's clothes. If you've always shopped at Anthropologie, shop at Anthropologie. We are not MAWs in any other decade but this one, and if Mick Jagger can still be siring offspring into his seventies, I can wear my scuffed cowboy boots well into mine.

And so can you.

Expert Tip: "I'm not sure I can pull off half of the stuff I just got on Amazon, but if I ever tell you that I bought anything cute at Chico's, you need to call the authorities. That's a distress signal. Also, my friend Brenna, who is in her midtwenties, told me that I can't be seen after dark in anything considered a blouse. I don't know what to do with that."—Vanessa Torre, MAW

Bonus Expert Tips: "Why are my ankles swollen? Because I drink too much wine."

"Do I have to shop at Chico's? Never. Unless you want to look like Carmella Soprano."—Lucia Macro, MAW

Knock, Knock.
Who's There?

I hadn't always been so positive about aging. There was a whole slew of stages that led to the epiphany that there is power and pride in making it past a half century. Before, I was just like Sara—offended and afraid. Those were some dark days. Days spent running from a future that I thought only promised prune juice and regular colonoscopies. There was the year I learned that Death's calling card makes no sound. I was haunted by it in ever-increasing frequency.

Perhaps I can spare you some of that grief. When it arrives at your doorstep, and it will, it sits patiently until you collect it and bring it inside.

And you will.

The card may rest, unnoticed, for several days or perhaps a shorter period of time, until you shuffle through it and, with either shock or curiosity, open the greeting.

You may believe that you will be able to hide from it, to lay low and remain unnoticed when the time comes, like waiting, terrified, until a giant spider passes over you in a nightmare, one leg creeping forward, then another. But don't be fooled. The spider knows you're there, and it understands that you believe yourself to have won. But you haven't. The spider will return in another dream, the one in which your ex-boyfriend tells everyone about the thinning spot on the crown of your head that you sometimes spray-paint or try to cover with extensions, and then starts repeating, "Laurie No-Back-Hair-O! Laurie No-Back-Hair-O!" until the entire crowd chimes in, including the spider, whom you didn't know was there until it leans down to rip your head off with its jaws like a grape from a ripe, juicy cluster.

Death's calling card looks innocent, plain, white, printed on unfussy paper. Standard stock, completely betraying what lies incubating inside it.

At first you might smile at the cheeriness of it all; it's a community, it will tell you. There are rewards. "Get ahead of whatever life has ahead," it will say coyly. "We're here to make your next steps easy, rewarding, and fun."

That's how Death hooks you—a brochure with photos of smiling retirees inside, the promise of another life, even better than the one you had before you held this envelope in your hands.

That's how Death waits and slips in. Just like that, it's done. With the tearing of an envelope, you have given your hand to him.

I have to stress, the calling card will always find you. No matter how many times you move, no matter how many times you get married, you can't escape. The universe has skip tracers better than rogue CIA agents. Rumors abound that Death's very envelope was found among Ted Kaczynski's things, soiled with drippings of canned stew and thick with the aroma of gasoline under a pair of wire cutters. But it was there.

It was there.

Before the calling card arrives, there are other ominous warnings that arrive by post. The morning I got the letter from Musgrove Mortuaries & Cemeteries encouraging me to buy a plot of land big enough to plant myself in, I just laughed and called them assholes. That mortuary had just torn down a stunning Craftsman mansion that had served as its business home for fifty years, then sold the land to Hilton, which built a prefab hotel on it that looked like a cargo ship from China barreling over the Atlantic toward all Walmarts great and small. As long as I was going to have to encounter that Hilton every time I left my house, I'd rather give my corpse to a body farm than give Musgrove the pleasure of letting me rot in their dirt.

As the first of my friends to turn fifty, I was surging into unknown territory. Sales pitches from mortuaries were just the first signs that I was moving into a strange, old land. I knew nothing of aging except what I'd observed, which, I learned later, was often obscured and falsely lit, like a Vegas magic act. The only hint of what lay ahead for me was when my mother blew out the candles on her birthday cake one year and announced, "I just made a promise to God that if he gave me my eyebrows back, I would never, ever pluck again."

And then, on the day that Death's calling card actually arrived, the beacon was lit. It was time for me to sail into unfamiliar seas, and I left the land of youth behind with no one to bid me farewell. Aging, it turns out, is contagious.

To this day, I have never opened Death's calling card. It arrives at my home no less than four times a year, often more, since I turned fifty. I must admit, it is sometimes tantalizing, proclaiming on the envelope vast discounts on cruises, oil changes, cheese baskets, and other things that younger people have no time for. But I will not succumb. Every time that the envelope marked "AARP" squats in my mailbox like a viper, it goes straight into recycling once discovered. What I invite in cannot hurt me, I believe.

AARP clearly knows of my disdain for them; they've countered my refusals to pay them attention by sending more and more calling cards, sometimes two in one day. The desperation to wrangle me into the AARP assisted-living cult was palpable;

I smirked every time I tossed a new bundle into my blue bin. But it didn't stop the onslaught. The frequency of the mailings became increasingly furious, and I didn't quite understand why until the day I actually looked at the envelope that I'd begun receiving in duplicate.

It was not addressed to me.

It was addressed to my husband. And it shouted, "WELCOME! Your membership details inside!"

I gasped. I had basically been a predator when, at thirty, I married my twenty-five-year-old husband. He was a baby. He could hardly grow a mustache. His skull bones were still fusing together when we walked down the aisle, and he believed every word I'd ever said to him.

My child bride.

How was this AARP outreach addressed to him? It wasn't possible!

When he came downstairs later that morning, I took a good, hard look at him.

Maybe . . . maybe that was not white cheddar powder in his beard but . . . just white whiskers?

Weren't those lines around his eyes indications of delight and happiness, or were they wear and tear from decades of grimacing and lack of a decent moisturizer?

"This is impossible," I said to myself. "My child bride has somehow become my geriatric bride?"

Then I caught sight of something that immediately washed all my fears away and circled them down the drain.

He was wearing Vans. The man was still wearing Vans, and I almost wept with relief. *You're still young*, I wanted to bellow as I stroked his white-cheddar beard. *You're still young!*

I saw that he had caught me staring at him, and I smiled.

"What's up?" he said with a questioning look.

"I was just admiring your skate punk shoes," I replied. "I didn't know you still had Vans."

He laughed. "Oh my God, are you kidding?" he replied. "I'll never give these up. I'll wear Vans until the day I die! I just got this pair!"

I grinned, relieved, and exhaled, the panic fading quickly away, like my fertility.

"Check 'em out!" my husband said, pulling up his pant leg so that I could get a full view of his sneaker glory.

And then it hit me like the last time I broke a toe. For only a moment, I knew what had happened, knew the consequences of what I was experiencing, but I was in that brief millisecond delay before the message reached my brain and pain thudded through.

He was wearing socks. My husband was wearing socks with his Vans. Like a grandpa.

There was nothing I could say. I marched into the kitchen, reached into the recycling bin, and carried the calling cards back to the living room, where I threw them at him.

"These are for you," I said, the AARP envelopes fluttering around him like dying doves.

He looked puzzled, then reached for one and broke into a broad smile.

"Oh my God," he said, waving it in the air. "I've been waiting for this!"

"Have fun with your new death cult," I said. "They may have gotten you, but they are not catching me. And if you think you're going to bring any of your new *old* friends home to have IcyHot parties, think again. Your AARP life is separate and apart from this one."

"But the discounts are so good!" he exclaimed.

"Discounts for what?" I asked, to which he responded by tearing open the envelope and flipping through.

"Walgreens," he declared, looking proud, "and fruit bouquets. And access to Pill ID!"

"That's awesome," I snapped back. "Have fun with your 30 percent off Epsom salts and fruit bouquets for sending to your friends when they find out they have cancer. And you already have a pill identifier in this house—me. Show it to me. I'll tell you what it is. Pink, yellow, white, oblong, capsule, round, whatever. If it's still lying around this house, it isn't any fun."

"I love fruit bouquets," he said. "Things on skewers are awesome. It's such a cheery way to say, 'I'm sorry you have a tumor, but here's a chunk of sunshine.' Plus, you get a free AARP day bag. I was hoping it would come today."

"You know that's to carry around your diapers, don't you?" I asked him. "It's not for snacks."

"It . . . could be for snacks," he said quietly.

"If you start throwing around the words *orthotics*, *buffet*, and *ointment*, you're going to need to find another place to live," I said. "You'll like your new home, though. It'll be the type of place that you can bring your diaper bag to, and they'll give you a necklace with a red button on it that you can push when you start seeing a mysterious bright light. You're going on this death trip alone, my friend. I'm not buying into the hype."

"That's the great thing," my husband said. "You don't have to buy anything! The AARP membership was 'buy one, get one free.' I signed you up for nothing!"

I suddenly saw a mysterious bright light, but I knew better than to think I was going to heaven, and I correctly identified the source as an anger flash, drawing me to certain extinction.

"No, you did not," I said adamantly. "You did not sell me out for a diaper bag!"

"No," he assured me. "I did not. Your welcome gift is a pair of grabbers that helps you put your socks on. You usually have to get a hip replacement before you can score one of those."

"Listen, buddy," I said staunchly. "You are new to this old game. I've been here now for a while. Don't be so eager to jump on every geriatric ride out there. You don't know the terrain. A newbie like you is prime for the picking."

"I don't know why you can't just be grateful," my husband shot back. "You probably have a good five years before you need a hip replacement. Can't you just be positive and think of it as an early Christmas present?"

I suppose some level of betrayal is expected in every marriage. I mean, there had been signs. Appearances changed. There were secret communications, and there was the onset of new health habits. It was all right there in front of me, but I hadn't put the pieces together. He'd bought shiny blue track pants with a stripe down the side that replaced his 501s. Recently, I'd found him collapsed on the floor, not moving but beet red, and I'd had to kick him several times before he showed any sign of life by gasping that he was just doing "yoga." And now there was his new pen pal, Death.

But when an *AARP* magazine arrived with what appeared to be Matthew McConaughey on the cover, there was no ignoring it. The movie star's eyes had pronounced bags, and his wrinkles were deeper than I had ever seen before. It looked like the heartthrob had been Photoshopped, but in reverse. Next to the headline "Finally, New Hope for Treating Strokes," McConaughey reached out his fingers as if he were going for a handful of granny boob.

Inside the magazine was a retrospective on MTV (Nina Blackwood is sixty-five and still has permed hair) and a piece about how dating after fifty is the best because you don't have to pick a mate who will be a good parent, and you can confidently request to see their financials. My blood ran cold as I realized that my only decent dating asset—wearing an underwire bra for forty-two years had paid off—paled in comparison to my FICA score, which I believed to be down in the double digits. "Would someone actually do that?" I gasped to myself, shifting an eye to my husband, who was on the ground mimicking a self-inflicted Abu Ghraib–stress position that was depicted on the following *AARP* page, entitled "Shake Your Hips!" But there was a much younger gentleman in the photo.

It was bad enough that in the '90s you had to tell people you were dating that you might have an STD. Now I'd have to disclose that I forgot to make a payment on my Bath & Body Works credit card?

True, my husband had given me up to the dark side—he had named my name—but he still has no idea that I have a Bath & Body Works credit card. And he never will.

"Please get up," I demanded. "According to your AARP bible, that pose is only good for false confessions and turning people in, and you've already done that for the promise of a Chinese-made diaper bag. Stop trying to put your foot behind your ear. In about twenty minutes, you're going to need more IcyHot than we have in this house. I'll buy you a day-of-the-week pillbox if you stop."

My husband unfurled himself as I watched, my panic rising.

"One with rainbow colors?" he asked. "Sometimes it's hard to read the print on the all-blue ones."

"Of course," I said. "Rainbow colors. We might even be able to get the days of the week in Braille."

"That would be helpful," he said earnestly.

Not long after, another calling card arrived. I saw the big red *AARP* sprawled across the top and huffed as I tossed it onto my husband's pile.

But then something caught my eye.

Jamie Lee Curtis was on the cover. I love Jamie Lee Curtis! I love that she is natural and honest, and that she posed for *More* magazine with no makeup and no styling, clad in only an exercise bra and panties to show what a woman's body really looks like. Even without Photoshop, fillers, or plastic surgery, she was rocking it.

Quietly, stealthily, like an old ninja, I took the magazine from his pile and secretly slid it under mine. If anyone was going to read about Jamie Lee Curtis, I was getting the first shot.

Anatomy of the Nightlife of a Lady

It was 2:43 a.m., and I was wide awake.

I wasn't a second ago. I had been sleeping, or at least I thought I was, and then, as if I had stuck a knife into a toaster, my body and consciousness flipped on. ON. A hundred and twenty watts ON.

Oh God. Not again.

Despite my newfound love of aging, some agonizing aspects remained. You never get a peach without a pit. Recent history notwithstanding, I continue to go to bed each night with the highest hopes. I snuggle into my king-size bed with my foam mattress topper, down comforter, and seven fluffy pillows.

That bed is the best place in the world.

And that is helpful, because I am awake most of the time I am there.

It all starts off so pleasantly. Earlier that night, I'd snuggled under the covers and started the procedure.

9:15 p.m.: one Klonopin (for restless leg syndrome).

One Sonata.

One Kirkland-brand oblong blue sleep aid.

Swallow.

Book or iPad? How lazy was I feeling? Did my eyes want to work, or did they just want to glaze over and watch *Homestead Rescue*?

In four minutes, I was looking on as Marty Raney and his two adult kids, Misty and Matt, descended upon a homestead in need of saving! The story is always the same: People invest their last fifteen thousand on forty acres in the Arizona desert with no access to electricity or, for that matter, water. But before you know it, sixtyish Marty rips off his shirt and begins waving a chain saw around like it's a fairy wand.

If I'm lucky, I get to the end of the episode without falling asleep on the iPad keyboard. Instead, an indeterminate amount of time later, I woke up when I heard Marty scream that Misty had been electrocuted or that Marty had chopped down a tree that landed on a homesteader's house. ("I have never had a tree fall on a house. And, for that, I apologize.") I'd been drooling on the keyboard, so I rewound until I got to see Misty getting electrocuted, then fell asleep once again before the end of the show.

11:15 p.m.: When I woke up a second time, I put the iPad away, turned off the light, and nestled into those seven pillows.

11:17 p.m.: Wide awake.

11:20 p.m.: Wide awake and mildly concerned that I would not be able to go back to sleep.

11:25 p.m.: Turned light back on. Riffled through bedside table until I found my sleep gummies. Took two. Turned off light.

11:27 p.m.: Turned on light. Found sleep gummies. Took another one. Started counting to a hundred, taking a deep breath and exhaling on each number. Lost track at thirty-two because if I hadn't fallen asleep already, I was not going to. Ever.

11:35 p.m.: *I need a cookie.*

11:39 p.m.: *I still need a cookie.*

11:40 p.m.: Went downstairs and got a cookie, then decided that I needed something salty to balance it. Ate half a pretzel, but the balance was off again, so ate another cookie.

11:45 p.m.: Went back upstairs. Got back into bed. Started counting over again.

11:47 p.m.: Decided counting was stupid and was keeping me awake. Tried to imagine myself sleeping on a cloud with a cool breeze lightly rippling over me. Focused. Focused. Focused.

11:51 p.m.: *OH MY GOD, I AM SO HOT. Why is it so hot in here? My husband is hogging the fan. There is no such thing as a hot cloud. I need to move to another cloud with a fan that is on me.* I kicked the sheet off, got up, moved the fan so it was blowing on me like a hurricane, and laid on my back with none of my limbs touching another part of my body. *I'm still hot. It is still so hot.*

2:15 a.m.: Eyes flew open. Was I awake? Had I been sleeping? My tongue was huge in my mouth and felt like sandpaper. I guzzled water from the bottle on the nightstand. The sheets were stuck to my arms. *Holy shit, did I pee myself? Oh my God. I am an animal. I am an old animal. I am going to have to lie in my own pee all night. My hair is even wet! Ohhhhhh, thank God, it's only night sweats. I can lie in sweat. I can totally lie in that kind of body fluid. Oh, thank you, God, thank you for not making it pee. I don't want pee hair. Thank you so much. But F you for messing with my hormones. I wonder how much estrogen I have left. I wonder how much just leaked out of my body and is now soaking my foam mattress topper. I bet my mattress topper is more of a lady now than I am. I am just a sexless log, sweating and counting like I'm learning English. I just want to sleep. Was I sleeping? Was I just lying here this whole time, sweating? My sleep gummies clearly aren't working. They never work. I have no idea why I take them. Time for the big guns.*

I reached over and turned on the light, fumbling for the bottle of gummies that were "a slipper for my brain." There is a big pot leaf on the label with an exclamation point, in case I ever mistake them for movie candy. They taste like shit, but it was 2:17 a.m., and I wanted to sleep. I needed a cough drop chaser and tried to rub it over the entire surface of my tongue. I counted to a hundred breathing in and breathing out, but I was afraid that if I fell asleep I'd choke on the cough drop and die.

I finally went ahead and chewed on the cough drop until it splintered into sharp shards in my mouth. *My toes hurt. Why do my toes hurt? They feel like little achy sausages. They are really hurting now. When is the brain slipper going to kick in? Ow. Ow, ow, ow. I'm never going to fall asleep if my toes hurt. Why do my toes hurt? Is there such a thing as toe cancer? Take my toes. I don't care. I just want sleep.*

2:32 a.m.: I remembered that there was IcyHot in the bathroom cabinet, and I peeled myself from the bed and headed down the hallway, running into the doorjamb in the dark. I fell over a little bit. I squinted into the bathroom cabinet for what seemed like hours. I finally found the white jar with a blue top and pulled it out, knocking toothpaste, dental floss, and a cascade of bobby pins into the sink. I flopped down on the closed toilet seat and massaged my little aching piggies with the foul ointment.

When I got back to bed, stinking like a huge Altoid, my foot got caught on the wet sheet, and the IcyHot wiped right off.

"What's that smell?" my husband mumbled from a deep, dark, deathlike sleep.

"Shut up," I said. My jealousy was overwhelming.

2:43 a.m.: An interminable gauntlet of pain began. I turned on my right side. My right hip hurt. I untangled myself from the wet sheets and turned on my left side. Bending my knee hurt. I turned onto my stomach and rammed my head into the pillow with my arm underneath it. In two seconds, my shoulder started throbbing. I took a deep breath and tried to flip myself in one motion, like a fish, onto my back. My toes hurt again. I turned on the lamp and fumbled through the nightstand drawer. I found a pill bottle coated with white powder on the inside, opened it up, and saw the last remnants of my past surgeries, injuries, and maladies. I saved these beauties for the densest of nights. I plucked one out, bit off half, and just chewed it, rubbing the surface of my molars with my tongue to make sure I got it *all*.

Then I felt it. The creepy-crawlies that descend upon my legs at nighttime and in movie theaters. I used to laugh at the idea of "restless leg syndrome," so *of course* now I had it.

I kept the urge to move at bay for as long as possible, but it felt like there were energy ants rushing inside my legs, which were desperate to jerk and twirl. They were full of electricity, and the more I tried to stay still, the worse it got until I wanted to scream. So I did kicks in bed, like a Rockette in a dirty T-shirt and underwear that should have retired years ago. It was ghastly. I did straight kicks and then knee kicks. I moved my ankles around in circles.

It was not enough. It was never enough. I had tried everything, including "folk" cures, to get my legs to calm down. I'd tried lotion. I'd tried magnets. I'd tried arnica gel for arthritic hands. But the only thing you can really do with restless legs is run them like horses.

I got out of bed and did some *Flashdance* moves. I ran in place, lunged, and flicked my ankles—left, right, left, right. If I hadn't already been soaked with sweat, that routine would have drenched me.

One, two, three. In and out. Four, five, six.

I was wide awake. Eyes wide open. *Bette Davis eyes. The eyes have it.*

2:55 a.m.: *Five hundred and sixty. Five hundred sixty-one. Five hundred sixty-two. Five hundred sixty-one.*

3:07 a.m.: *I wonder what Marty Raney is doing right now. Seeing Misty get electrocuted was wild. She just flew across the roof in an L shape, her legs sticking out in front of her torso. That was funny. She was fine and didn't get hurt, so it's okay to laugh. Totally okay to laugh.*

I reached over and grabbed my iPad from the nightstand, then turned the lamp on. My husband grunted and pulled the comforter over his head.

"Shit up," I replied. "I mean, shut up."

I opened the iPad and entered my passcode. I knew this code like I knew my birthday, so it was annoying that it still wasn't letting me in after five tries. Finally, I got access. But, um. What channel was *Homestead Rescue* on? Hulu? Discovery? HGTV? Peacock? I opened Hulu first, but the show didn't pop up, so I entered "Himaestead rescc" into the field, and it said they didn't have a show like that. *Whatever. I'll try—I'll try—what was the other one? Hulu? I'll try Hulu next.* But then I couldn't find the Hulu icon after going through five pages of apps. I found Discovery, and after I hit the icon several times, the screen started to shake, and I focused very hard to really target my poke at Discovery, and it took a couple of times before the app vanished and the screen stopped shaking. *Whatever.*

My husband threw the comforter off. He was lying on his back with a CPAP locked on his face, like a crab with an elephant's trunk. I wished I had a peanut so that I could stick it in the end and watch as it got sucked up. Instead, I opened another app, which worked this time, aimed the tablet, and snapped a picture. "This is revenge," I whispered at his sleeping body. "This is what you get for taking a picture of me after I ate a doughnut and fell into a sugar coma with my tongue sticking out."

I was about to post the picture to Facebook when I noticed that my friend Liska had posted a minute ago that she'd just eaten a bowl of cereal. That my friend Amy had just finished painting her toenails and eating a protein bar. That my friend Liz had given up on trying to sleep and was posting videos of puppies that were not hers.

We were all there. All the ladies were there. None of us could sleep, and we were all on Facebook.

"I've taken enough sleeping pills to kill Judy Garland seventeen times over," I posted. "And I'm still awake."

"If Judy Garland had waited until menopause to OD, she'd still be alive," my friend Erica wrote back. "If anyone has a tranquilizer dart gun for an elephant, I'll give you a hundred bucks to come and shoot me through my window."

"I haven't slept since 2018," Lore posted. "And I just finished the last episode of *Homestead Rescue*. I have NyQuil decanted on my nightstand. Even that can't conquer me."

"I hate protein bars," Amy wrote. "I'm going to make a cake. And then I'm going to ravage it without using my hands."

"I'm in a women's writing circle, and we took a poll," Michelle said. "All twelve of us are on pot gummies."

"We're all on pot gummies," Erica agreed. "Middle-aged women and pizza delivery guys are keeping the industry alive."

"Even my mother takes pot gummies," Judy added.

I thought about an unidentified mother I know who also takes pot gummies at night, even though she voted to keep it illegal after she got her card. "I don't want to see a whole generation hopped up on pot!" this woman had explained to me.

Well, the evidence tonight shows that there is a whole generation hopped up on pot, I telepathed to the unidentified mother of someone I know, *and it includes you*.

None of us could sleep, but at least we were getting stuff done. We were baking cakes! Painting our toenails! Learning how to survive on a homestead! It took me until middle age to learn how to properly chop a tree down, how to build a bear-proof chicken coop, and how to build an outhouse thirty feet in the air. My neighbor Sarah reads an entire book a night. You can tell if a young mother or father has been up all night with their kids—actually, you don't even have to be a detective, because they'll tell you the first time you see them that day. "Two kids sick and another kicked me all night," they mumble. "Need more coffee." Yet, the entire population of middle-aged women are showing up to work on three hours of sleep (some with their night meds still coursing through their bloodstream), running meetings, making deadlines, and putting curses on their bosses. (It was just a little packet of dirt from a graveyard sprinkled in their office.) And the rest of the world has no idea. Why? Because we are superwomen. Because it's how we are. We're high, we're sleep deprived, and we're still doing all the shit. If my husband doesn't get his full eight hours, he'll mention it the whole next day, as if he spent the dark time keeping flesh-eating zombies from gaining entry to our house. Not middle-aged women. They get up from a bed they've never slept in, put on an underwire and some mascara, and do it all over again. And no one knows.

That night, I exchanged a couple of recipes, taught an audience how to make a one-minute alfredo sauce, heard the entire plots of three movies that I hadn't had time to see (only because theaters close at the amateur hour of midnight), and enjoyed Amy's cake virtually.

It was a great party, but I had to go to sleep. I wanted to go to sleep. I was so very tired. I wandered into the kitchen and looked through the pantry, wondering what I should scarf down next. I opened the refrigerator and scanned that too.

It was then that I had my brilliant idea. My nephew and his friends had recently come to visit, and they had plundered our booze supply, filling all the bottles up with water—a trick every generation thinks they are the first to invent. But there was one bottle they hadn't touched: the Kahlúa.

Fools.

I'd discovered the drink in my high-school years, when my friends and I would go to a French café and somehow not get carded, even though we still looked like fifth graders.

"Kahlúa and cream," we'd say, feeling so sophisticated and mature. "And quiche."

Now, there I was, forty years later, standing in my kitchen in a T-shirt, exhausted from kicking like a stallion, night sweats finally evaporating, pouring a coffee mug halfway full of liqueur and then finishing it off with a hearty gulp of nondairy, sugar-free Italian Sweet Crème Coffee mate.

How the mighty had fallen.

I'd almost finished it in two gulps when something on the counter caught my eye. A little pill bottle. Full of tiny tramadols. With my dog's name on it.

YES, I DID.

I stole painkillers from my dying, cancer-ridden dog.

I can get more, my brain slurred.

I used the last gulps of Kahlúa and Coffee mate to wash down the pill, and then for good measure (and because my dog weighs a third of what I do), I popped another one, turned off the light, and stumbled up the stairs to bed.

"Honey, honey," I heard my husband say as he shook my foot. "Coffee is ready."

The sun was up, but it felt like I had only slid into bed fifteen minutes before.

"Shut up," I whispered.

"I will in a minute," he replied. "Right after you tell me why there is a picture of me and my CPAP all over Facebook."

Death or Cake

I wasn't expecting to spend Easter Sunday under my dining room table with six strange men observing as the seventh cut my panties off with an enormous pair of scissors.

Although I knew my husband was there, I couldn't see him. He was somewhere behind the guy who was trying to get the fountain of blood to stop shooting out of my thigh. I just hoped my husband had stopped crying.

I have a standard line I use in humiliating situations—"I usually get paid for a show like this"—but I'd crossed into a territory of humiliation that was too awful for jokes. I was naked from the waist down, and my hands were dark brown, smeared with the blood that was soaking through my Pottery Barn rug.

It could be worse, I thought weakly to myself. *At least it's not a Restoration Hardware rug.*

Only an hour before, I had put a blueberry Bundt cake into the oven. My husband and I had been invited over by our friends Mary and Bennet, and I had planned ahead so that the cake would be done in plenty of time.

As it baked, that cake smelled so good. Wafts of buttery crumb mixed with farmers-market blueberries made both my and my husband's mouths water. When the timer went off, I carefully pulled it out of the oven, astonished at what I had accomplished. Truth be told, I'm not the best baker. My cookies burn, my cakes go lopsided because of my eighty-year-old oven, or my hair ends up in the batter. This happens so often that I used to tell my nephews, "If you find the Lucky Hair in your food, that means you get extra ice cream," and on more than one occasion, there would be a sad little face accompanied by a whimpering, "I didn't get the Lucky Hair."

But this cake? It was a masterpiece—golden brown on top, popping with blueberries on the surface, and it smelled delightful. I did the right thing, and instead of turning it onto the cake dish immediately and watching it crumble into a Bundt landslide, I let it cool on the counter for half an hour. I was impressed with my work and was sure that everyone else at Easter dinner would be as well.

After half an hour had passed, I touched the cake lightly, and it had cooled.

"It's time!" I said to myself triumphantly.

I fetched the domed glass cake plate (Martha Stewart brand) from the kitchen nook table and headed toward the counter. But my house is old, as in a century old, and in certain places, the floor bounces. In fact, it bounces a lot when a middle-aged chunk is racing to plate her glorious cake, and in this case the vibration was enough to cause a broom to topple over and catch my foot. I tripped, sending the heavy cake plate shooting through the air.

I saw it go. I saw it fly feet ahead, surging with the g-force of a carnival ride operated by a tweaker who hasn't slept in three days. In a fraction of a second, I watched as it toppled back to earth, where it splintered into a thousand sparkly shards like a spray of diamonds.

As I looked at it, I couldn't help but think, *That is going to slice my face up like a loaf of bread*. And then . . . I was down.

I hit the kitchen floor with a dense thud, the air forced out of my lungs, as my hands didn't even have time to reach out and brace the fall.

I gasped, struggling to gather a breath. Miraculously, my face was up, off the floor, intact.

Oh my God, I thought, *I'm okay. I'm really okay.* I couldn't believe it. I could breathe again, and I was fine. Nothing hurt. I was totally fine. *I'm so lucky, I'm so lucky, I'm so lucky*, I said over and over in my head.

And then I felt it. Not a trickle. Not a stream. But a gush of something warm and forceful on my thigh, and then down my leg.

Then I was standing, I don't know how, but I was, and I looked down and said in slow motion, "Ohhhhh fuuuuucccckkkkkkk . . ."

I know where my arteries are. I can't divide thirty-five by seven correctly, but I know where my arteries are. And blood was pouring out of my femoral artery like it was a gas pump that had fallen out of a car's tank.

I have three minutes to live, I realized.

My husband was suddenly in the kitchen, watching blood pool around my feet.

"Nine-one-one?" he said, and I nodded.

I pushed with everything I had, both hands on the source of the spill. I pushed and pushed and pushed.

"Get on the floor," my husband said, grabbing my arm.

He pulled out a dining room chair and flung it aside with one hand as his other held the phone and pushed me onto the floor.

He put the phone on speaker and used both hands to press a towel on my thigh, all his weight on the Moby Dick spout that was literally shooting vertically into the air.

"Sir," I heard a tinny voice say, "keep her talking! I don't hear her talking!"

"You're doing a good job, honey," I said loud enough to hear.

"Has the bleeding stopped?" the voice asked.

"No," my husband said. "I can't get it to stop."

"They are almost there, sir," the voice said.

"The front door is locked," I told my husband. "You need to open it."

"Do not leave, sir," the voice insisted. "Keep the pressure on. Do not leave her. They'll get in."

I looked at my husband. I didn't feel any pain. But the towel was getting redder, and so was my husband's face. He was sweating. A lot. Trails of sweat were running from his eyes down his cheeks. I looked at him, puzzled, and then I realized it wasn't sweat.

"It's going to be fine," I assured him. "I'm fine. I don't feel anything. I'm really okay."

"I'm pushing as hard as I can," my husband said.

"You're doing really great," I said, as if he was giving birth.

"Keep the pressure on, sir," the phone voice said. "Do not let up on that pressure."

And then, suddenly, my dining room was full of men. Firemen, or firepeople, or whatever we're supposed to call them now. Fire personnel. I don't know. But I saw their boots, their yellow rubber pants, and my husband was gone. Then so were my pants, and my underwear was about to be sliced away from my lady parts.

"I'm so sorry," I apologized. "I've been married for twenty-five years. My razors are older than my car. I'm so sorry. I would have tidied up had I known that the Eugene Fire Department was going to witness an unveiling today."

No one said anything, which I took to be a very bad sign, but I didn't have too much time to dwell on it. I was on a stretcher being wheeled out in front of my neighbors, who were all gathered on the street. Someone had the good sense to cover my bottom half with a blanket, but when I waved my Ted Bundy bloody hands to say goodbye, their jaws dropped, and there was silence as the ambulance doors closed at my feet.

The sirens blared, which seemed like another bad sign, and someone asked me to sign a paper saying I was okay with getting a transfusion.

"Are you giving me one now?" I asked as I signed, leaving a blood trail on the form.

"We'll see," the paramedic said.

"I think I got my femoral artery," I added, hoping that my insight as a nonmedical professional might help the medical professional sitting beside me.

"Maybe," he said. "We won't be able to tell until we get in there."

"Oh," I said and then got up the nerve to ask, "Am I going to bleed out?"

And that, my friends, got no response.

I didn't bargain. I didn't plead like I might have in earlier stages of my life. I got mad.

I can't believe this, I rage-thought to myself. *If I die half naked and bloody because I made a cake, I am going to . . . actually, that's a pretty good story.*

Too bad I won't be around to tell it.

I didn't ask any more questions after that. Once we arrived at the hospital, the door wasn't even open before the paramedic looked at me and said, "Now I can tell you that you're not going to bleed out."

As I was rolled into the ER, a flock of nurses and assistants and doctors descended upon me.

"What happened?" asked one of them.

"I fell on a cake plate," I replied.

"What?"

"I fell on a cake plate."

"This is what happened," one of the paramedics said and held up his iPhone.

"Whoa," the doctor said.

"What is that?" I asked.

"It's the shard of glass that impaled you," he said and then showed me the photo.

What I saw on his phone was a large, curved sword of glass with a glistening pool of blood sitting in the belly of it.

"I was impaled?"

"Looks like it," said the man, beginning to unwrap the makeshift bandage around my thigh. "Does it hurt?"

I was honest. "Not really. I mean, I know it's there, but I thought it would hurt a lot more."

"It's five inches wide," he told me. "And—"

Before he could finish, I screamed the F word because it felt like someone had just stuck a hot iron right into that wound, except it turned out that it was just the doctor searching around inside my leg for other pieces of glass.

"You owe me some Dilaudid for that one, buddy," I said, trying to catch my breath. "Do not do that again."

And then a goddess appeared with an IV bag hanging from her widespread steel arms. Within seconds, someone hooked me up, and then . . .

And then . . .

And then . . .

Warm, slow honey swam up my arm, so beautiful, so golden, so calm. So gorgeous. In the center of my chest, petal by petal, I felt a flower bloom with a patient, steady glow of unfiltered glory until it unfurled into an ocean of peace.

It was, without a doubt, the best moment of my life.

Thank God my parents only gave me a seventy-dollar allowance when I was in college, which I mainly blew on booze and cigarettes. This kind of love had been out of my price range.

After that, I didn't really care what they did to me. I was showing off my hands and exclaiming, "Can you believe how much blood came out of me? This is like Manson-family shit."

As if that wasn't a big enough gift, a surgeon swept into the ER bay and held out her hand.

"I'm Dr. Henderson," she said. "I'm pretty sure I'm going to be doing surgery on your leg today."

I gasped with joy. "Dr. Henderson! OH MY GOD!!! It's me, Laurie Notaro! Do you remember? I had that crazy tumor?"

Dr. Henderson shook her head. "I'm sorry."

"You took that tumor out of my neck, remember? It was growing around my lung, and you had to have another doctor friend help you pull it out? You had your hand all the way inside my back? Remember? It was circus-size?"

She thought for a minute. "Did I take a picture of it for my book of oddities to show my students?"

"Yes!" I exclaimed and reached forward to hug her with my serial-killer arms, but she smiled and retreated. "And I put *you* in *my* book, too, so we're even!"

She smiled politely, as you do at a half-naked woman who is as high as Robert Downey Jr. was in the '90s. As she hovered over my leg, I asked her how deep she thought the wound was. Without flinching, she held up her gloved hand, the entire length of her fingers covered in blood.

"That's a good three inches deep," she said. "But that glass was really thick. I can try to stitch it up right now, or we can do sur—"

"Surgery!" I cried. "Definitely surgery. That. That. Please do surgery. I would like surgery, please."

"I think that's a good choice," she agreed, most likely because she wanted me to stop talking.

They packed the impalement site with gauze and wheeled me upstairs to surgery. A very nice nurse took a sponge and began to wipe the blood off my feet.

I started to laugh. "It's Easter, and this is just like Mary Magdalene washing Jesus's feet!"

The nurse looked at me, aghast. I was the only one laughing.

"We're in a Catholic hospital," my husband hissed at me.

"I used to be Catholic before I learned about science," I offered, trying to soften the offense.

When I saw Dr. Henderson again in the operating room, I didn't even have time to mention my circus tumor or reach for another hug before I was unconscious.

I woke up hours later; I really don't remember where. Someplace in a Catholic hospital where I was not making friends successfully.

My husband was next to me and quickly gave me the details. "Five inches wide, three inches deep. She had to sew you up in three layers. You were a quarter inch away from the artery. The glass didn't hit the bone, but it was close. And nerves were severed. Her exact words were, 'The meat was all cut.'"

I absorbed that for a moment, still in the thick swirl of anesthesia.

"Will I—" I whispered, my mouth thick with cottony dryness. "Will I—"

"Of course you'll walk again," my husband said. "Don't be stupid. But do you want to stay overnight? They'll give you IV pain meds if you do."

"I will stay here forever if they keep me hooked up to that thing," I whispered back.

"That's what I told them," he replied. "Here's a text from your sister."

He showed me the screen, and on it was a primitive drawing of me on the ground with no pants, blood squirting out of my leg, my dog eating the cake, and tears flying from my husband's face. Beneath it was a message: "We love you, Aunt Laurie!"

"How did she know you were crying?" I asked.

"I told her," he said.

When I got home the next day, my husband showed me the pile of glass he had swept together but not thrown away. Resting on top was an enormous crescent-shaped stake, jagged, half an inch thick, and coated with dried blood. It was the same piece of glass that the paramedic had shown me a photo of.

"Well, now that you've seen the instrument of near death, let's get rid of it," my husband said, pitching it into the trash.

"Oh hell no!" I said, attempting to snatch the trash bag out of his hand. "That thing tried to kill me, and I survived! It's my talisman!"

"You are not keeping it," my husband informed me. "There's no way I'm ever going to rule out you falling on it again. Do you want me to say it again? *The meat was all cut.*"

"Not only am I keeping it," I insisted, "but that baby is going to be mounted on our living room wall like a trophy kill."

"At least clean the blood off," he pleaded.

"No way," I declared. "I'm dipping this relic into a vat of polyurethane. I'll be on this thing forever and ever and ever."

My husband shook his head and put the bag down. "You're also going to have one hell of a scar."

"I know," I said sadly. "The only way I can show it off is to start dating again."

"Do you remember that I cried?" he replied.

"Very sweet," I said, then motioned to the Bundt pan still on the kitchen counter. "For now, let us eat cake."

Help!

The truth is, I knew better. Before I even registered at Nextdoor.com, I had bad things in mind.

I only ventured onto the site because my neighbor Sarah told me that she had been in a fight with a local woman who was stealing other people's cats and had been caught on video. The clip, Sarah said, was on Nextdoor.com and was hilarious.

As a woman who has lived long enough to know myself, I do *try* to stay away from such sites. I've been kicked off Yelp and banned from Craigslist. I have actively blocked at least five hundred people on Facebook. The brilliance of growing older is that with each passing day, you lose an equivalent amount of fear. I have less tolerance for unexperienced voices who think they know more than a person twice their age, and I'm not afraid to say so. My husband says that this will eventually lead to rifle shot flying through my gut, and he's probably right, but if a girl in her twenties who is in the same Facebook group as me thinks that I'm discriminating against the entirety of Italian American culture because I posted that a red gingham dress looked like a tablecloth from Buca di Beppo, someone has to teach her something. There are two things people in their twenties do better than anyone else: get drunk and fall down and experience unplanned pregnancies. That, Greta, is your specialty. That is your area of expertise, dear girl, not calling other women out for failing to be tablecloth woke. Save it, and get another day of life under your belt before you start acting like you're older than you are.

So did this fearless middle-aged woman go into the Nextdoor.com abyss with genuinely bad intentions? Not exactly. After I saw the cat lady stealing a cat that wasn't hers, I decided to poke around a little on our "Friendly Neighborhood" (that's really the name). There were several posts by people who wanted everyone to slow down when driving on their street, or park differently on their street, or throw their trash out somewhere other than their street. There were the typical missing pet posts. There was an offer for a queen-size mattress with a picture of it posed in the middle of the street. There was a woman who was pissed that her neighbors were chopping down their trees, and a video of a water leak at Jefferson and Twenty-Fourth that was so shaky and panicked, I expected to see Bigfoot peek out from behind a light post. There was also a lady who was offering to pick up some lucky person's dog's poo for twenty dollars a day, and another who needed to borrow space in someone's freezer for "two to three hours."

I resisted asking the guy with the mattress about the origins of the dark stain on it. And telling the woman that trees were most likely being cut down because of fire perimeters (since our town had nearly burned to the ground a year before). And suggesting that the poo lady should probably charge by weight. And offering room in my freezer for a foot and maybe a hand. I even resisted asking, "Might anyone know where I can forage some morels?"

I considered this a very strong streak of resistance, but that self-control came crashing down when I read the below.

> **Dear Friendly Area Neighbors**: I was out for a beautiful walk today down our lovely streets, and it could not have been more perfect. I was breathing in the scent of flowers and fresh air when, suddenly, I was assaulted by the stink of a scented dryer sheet, which has been proven to cause cancer and ruined my walk immediately. STOP USING DRYER SHEETS! You are KILLING your neighbors!

Now, I live in Eugene, Oregon, where people are so far to the left that they have almost looped around again to the right, and they have no problem demanding that other people not ruin their nature walks by doing laundry. This attitude is super typical of the neighborhood. We are liberated and free! We delight in passing that liberation on to others by telling everyone else exactly how to live.

I have few friends in Eugene, and that is fine by me. My dance card is full. I'll turn a blind eye to someone putting Styrofoam in their recycling, although if you have chickens and you aren't cleaning up after them, you can count on me to turn you in to the authorities. It took only one rat running along my yard fence for that phone call to be made, followed by fifteen subsequent calls until the ordinance compliance officer for the city finally agreed to dump industrial rat birth control into the sewers on my street. Again, we're so left that we cannot kill rats, but we will provide free Plan B to combat the results of unbound rat love.

But the dryer-sheet post on Nextdoor got me. It had already garnered 126 comments—a record, according to one neighbor—by the time I saw it. The original poster explained that Snuggle dryer sheets were not FDA approved for human consumption, but "human consumption" was exactly what happened when any one of us breathed in the sweet scent of Snuggle. Fights broke out in the comments about whose air was being contaminated. Is the air on someone's property public air or private air? Who owns air? Can you sue for being forced to breathe in Snuggle? It went on and on, and, frankly, I started to wonder if everyone in my town is retired but me, because they sure seemed to have a lot of time on their hands to argue about the scent of fresh linen and lavender.

Then, before I knew it, my fingers were flying, and I hit "Return."

"Help!" my headline read. I posted it in the "Safety" section of the website. "People have been walking in front of my house. This must stop. It's driving my dog crazy."

The thing is, it's true. My dog barks at everything—she's a great watchdog, but sometimes the barking reaches a point where I just want to give her a sedative and then pop one for myself. We have a lot of pedestrian traffic on our street, perhaps even the Snuggler, and it's a nonstop bark parade at my house.

I figured that my post would let off a little steam for me and then die a lonely death because it was so ridiculous. But within fifteen seconds, I had a bite.

> **Jeanette B.:** Do you live in town? With a sidewalk in front of your house? People can't be expected to take a longer route to get where they want to go. That's what sidewalks are for. Maybe you need to train your dog. If you can't, hire a dog trainer. Or move out of town.

At seventeen seconds, another one appeared.

Lisa D.: This is a dog-friendly community. People walk their dogs at all times, and dogs tend to stretch the bounds of leashes. Maybe this is what is happening. Dogs are venturing upon your front lawn. It is likely not ill-minded intent of behavior, on the animal's or person's part. But I have to agree with the abovementioned. Seek to control your dog, and not the society to which you are a member of.

Wow! I thought to myself. *This could be fun.*

Laurie Notaro: Yes, I do have a sidewalk, approximately fifty feet of it. But it's my sidewalk. I can prove that because the city made me pay to fix the cracks in it. I am responsible for it, so it is a private sidewalk. And I really don't like people I don't know in front of my house.

Marshall K.: It's generally considered a good sign when people are seen walking in a neighborhood rather than having empty streets lined by closed garage doors. It's a healthy sign of life and social intercourse.

Your dog is probably more of a disruption or danger than anyone strolling past your house.

These people were just handing me gold.

Laurie Notaro: Marshall: I definitely don't want intercourse in front of my house. That is exactly what I'm trying to avoid!

Meadow S.: Is this post for real? Not an early April Fools' joke? Wow, I really need to quit this site.

Marshall K.: You are not comprehending the definition of "social intercourse."

Erin C.: Laurie, perhaps if you leave a bunch of dog poop on the sidewalk in front of your own house, people will begin to avoid your sidewalk. You know, mark your territory . . .

Laurie Notaro: Marshall: Social intercourse means more than one person. I just looked it up. And that is just disgusting.

Lisa D.: They make you pay for repair, for different reasons. Not because of ownership of the property of sidewalk. You know how living in cities works? Like requiring people to build with material that is nonflammable. The city requires this, but does not pay for it. Sidewalks and damages too.

Bob F.: Couple of things. First, homeowners are responsible for maintaining sidewalks, but that does not mean they own the sidewalk (see regulation here https://www.eugene-or.gov/FAQ.aspx?QID=306). Dog training is also an option, but sometimes it is an issue with the breed of dog itself, which might be wrong for this setting or these circumstances. Labradors chase balls and some breeds are very territorial. It is just what they are and do. Which, like the sidewalk, falls on the dog owner.

Laurie Notaro: Lisa: You know the law that says if you broke it, you bought it? Buying means owning. Therefore, I own my sidewalk. I should have a say about who is in close proximity to my house. Sometimes, people are even running, and I live on a hill, so when they are running from uphill, it makes a tremendous amount of noise. That is very bothersome, especially if they have big feet.

Laurie Notaro: Bob: See above. I'm afraid the regulation is wrong. And I took my dog to PetSmart, so she is well trained. Any dog that doesn't bark when predators are in front of their house is an ill-trained dog.

Marshall K.: Laurie . . . have you thought about building a wall to keep out all those predators? Of course, I suppose some are good people.

Laurie Notaro: Marshall: Thank you! You are exactly right; I think a wall might solve some of the problems, but honestly, I think a toll sidewalk would be better. I don't think asking people for a dollar to walk on my sidewalk is out of the question.

Mike W.: Have you considered building a big beautiful wall blocking the sidewalk and making pedestrians pay for it?

Sheri S.: Sorry, but oh good lord! It's come to this now?

Laurie Notaro: Mike W., we are singing the same song, my friend. I don't think I should bite off too much at once, starting with a toll gate. I'm also thinking I might run my dryer all the time with fabric softener sheets in it as a scent barrier to keep people away, but then again, that defeats the purpose of the toll. Any suggestions?

Jeffrey C.: Laurie, as a city of Eugene employee who managed trees in the Right of Way, I can hopefully shed some light on your issue with the sidewalk. As mentioned above, the sidewalk is the responsibility of the adjacent homeowner. Sidewalks tend to exist in the right of way for the use of pedestrians. I would recommend checking to verify the sidewalk is actually in the right of way strip, but ultimately there is nothing you can do about people using the sidewalk. They are supposed to provide safe passage for people to not have to walk in the street, and they are required to be ADA accessible, which is a federal requirement. Like the sidewalk, the vegetation in the right of way is homeowner responsibility, except for the trees, which are managed as a public utility. If you think the sidewalk should be managed the same way instead of privately, bring it up with city council and have a conversation about city code. If you're questioning the Public Right of Way, call the sidewalk inspector at the City of Eugene Public Works department.

Jeanette B.: Laurie, no, it's not your sidewalk. Talk to the city. You are responsible for keeping it and the parking strip in good shape, but the city owns it. It's public property. I had to pay $600 to repair the sidewalk in front of my house as well. But it's the public's right to use it.

Laurie Notaro: Again, I state the well-known law of you pay for it, you own it. I VOTED

FOR THAT LAW. I did talk to the city, and they told me to pay for it, so it's mine. Even stephen. I even pay to have the strip of grass on the other side of the sidewalk mowed, so there's that proof too. I get an invoice every month from the lawn company. I also want to outlaw large trucks and bicycles.

Dante Douglas: Biking is just walking with round feet . . . "No thanks!" Buy a Prius if you want to move places.

Laurie Notaro: Dante: I DO have a Prius! Now that's a car I don't mind driving in front of my house. Very quiet. Very quiet. Sometimes it's so quiet that I have to stop and yell at squirrels to get out of the way. Priuses have become the number one natural enemy of squirrels, I read.

Laurie Notaro: Cheryl: Someone is walking in front of my house right now, and my dog is barking like crazy! It's an old man, so he's moving very slow and making her bark even louder. She is being TORMENTED. This is PRECISELY what I'm talking about!

Terri T.: What kind of dog do you have? I have a buzzing bark collar you can borrow if you'd like. It doesn't zap the dog. Just buzzes. Anyway, let me know if you're interested in borrowing the bark collar.

Jonathan J.: I am really starting to think the wall might be a great idea.

Laurie Notaro: Terri: It was very kind of you to offer the buzz collar so I could electrocute my dog a little bit.

Aabc Eugene: Ah, the Idiot Girl strikes again.

And right here, I thought the jig was up. I had been identified, and now my house of cards was going to come careening down. But it turns out that people really don't read the comments. They only really care about their own response to your post.

Jennifer S.: I just want to say, I can relate to your problem. Loud cars used to drive past my house during the day when my children were babies and wake them up from their naps. Or even more often, people would park on my street and slam their car doors closed when they disembarked. The thoughtlessness drove me crazy! Didn't they know there could be sleeping babies??!! Shhhhh . . .

Fat Kid: I offer to patrol your private sidewalk and prevent intruders-by. I would only ask for $15/hr.

Sera P.: QUESTION!!! Is this whole post about a lady who has no business having a dog or access to the internet, or is it a subtle political discussion about Trump's Wall? Seriously I'm asking cuz both seem pretty accurate by the comments.

Tony U.: Please sign my 5,000 strong Change.org petition to stop people from walking. Walking must be stopped.

Cat I.: Dryer Sheets 125 vs. Sidewalks 117 . . . They're neck and neck at the final quarter . . .

Deb K.: Since you can't build a wall in front cuz city code, just put up stakes and string a wire and hang dryer sheets on it. Call it art and they can't make you take it down. Encourage others to add their own dryer sheets to it and pretty soon no one will walk or drive by your house.

Aryana F.: You know, the only thing that bothers me about this post is the typical self-righteous attitude that so many Eugenians carry, that is expressed in great quantities here. It is the one reason I have never really enjoyed living here. Everyone thinks they know the best way to live, think, and be (based of course on what works so well for them and so if it is true for them, well then it must be true for everyone else) when generally they have no clue about anyone else's life that they are judging, be it through humor or not. Humor in my book is about ironies in life, not making fun of those you don't understand.

Laurie Notaro: There is nothing quite like a diatribe about self-righteousness, is there? But with that post, I think we beat Dryer Sheets!

Michael C.: While you may have topped the Dryer Sheets, you still have a long way to go before you challenge the Elderly Woman Driving a Blue Taurus post.

Chad S.: Claymores and a couple .50 caliber machine guns would keep those pesky pedestrians and their dogs away from "your" sidewalk.

All in all, I think we had a pretty good run. By the time someone brought up firearms, we had beat out the Snuggler by five comments, which I will call a victory. I will never know if the Snuggler was a real person or someone who wanted to rattle the Eugene community to its very core, but either way, I have to admit that I am jealous of not thinking of the laundry air pollution scenario first.

I put the thread to sleep, because once someone starts talking military artillery and destruction and death, it's akin to peeing in the pool. Everyone gets out screaming and runs to their mom to towel off. Of course, no thread is really complete without the verifiably untrue phrase "we are better than this," which the thread clearly proved was not true. No one is better than complaining about dryer sheets and threatening to build a toll bridge in front of their house, and no one is better than complaining about that complaint.

Now, although I had a great deal of fun one evening seeing how far I could push the ridiculousness of Eugene's Nextdoor righteousness, I'm no social scientist. All I know is that people can get pretty bent out of shape despite all the yoga studios, the incredibly high percentage of strip-mall Reiki masters, and the abundance of Rolfers in this place. You want to float in complete darkness in a water tank that hasn't been cleaned since it was installed (and that I can say with utmost certainty has been peed in)? This is your town. Find your chakra balance in a black pee pool, and when you're done, go on Nextdoor.com to rattle off some city ordinance regulations just for the shit of it. I hadn't uncovered any deep truths about my community, but I'd had fun. It was time to move on.

But the post and its record-breaking responses had not, in fact, died.

"YOU'VE GONE VIRAL" was the title of an email that my boss, Jennifer, sent me one morning. I opened the email, and there was a link to a Twitter account called "Best of Nextdoor. com." I clicked it, and there before my eyes was "Help! People have been walking in front of my house. This must stop."

I didn't even know that Jennifer had seen the original post, but now we had sort of, kind of, become what my students call "Twitter famous." I didn't know whether to squeal from joy or actually build that wall around my house in case it caught the eye of some internet lurker with a grudge.

The Twitter-famous buzz lasted for a flash, and then it was over. Frankly, it was a little disappointing. I had envisioned news teams spilling over my Twitter-famous sidewalk, and cameras rolling to capture a glimpse of me and the sound of my tormented dog, but none of that happened. Coca-Cola wouldn't buy the rights to my post. There would be no TV movie. No guest spot on *Ellen*. A few more million would be added to the list of people who think I am insane, and that was it.

As time passed, I forgot about the post. I stopped telling the story at parties, my husband walking quickly away from me as I bellowed, "When someone shows up with .50 caliber machine guns, it's time to shut the bitch down." Even my people on Nextdoor.com didn't recognize my name when I went head-to-head with an urban chicken farmer up the street who denied that keeping chickens attracts rats. (Note: they do, and I posted a link to the *New York Times* story that proves it.)

Then, earlier this year, I was messing around online, and a teaser ad for Buzzfeed popped up, yelling "17 Screenshots of the Top Nextdoor.com Posts." I was chomping at the bit to see if people in other neighborhoods of the world were as touchy as mine, and I was disappointed to see that the number one post on the list was not the Snuggler but, instead, someone who lived in Windsor Park West asking, "Loud boom? Anyone else hear a loud boom?"

What does that even mean? I asked myself.

Surely, surely, the Snuggler was a higher karat of gold than Loud Boom?

Shaking my head at the undeserved win, I moved on to the second-place winner and gasped. For a moment, the world tilted, expanded, shrank, and then jigged a little bit.

My last name was blurred out, but "Friendly Area" was not, and my post read exactly as I had written it. On the internet. *For billions of people to see.*

I never expected to win a Pulitzer or a National Book Award, but . . . *this*? This was amazing! Buzzfeed had identified my post as the runner-up to that of Loud Boom. Unbelievable! The honor. The honor!

I didn't know who to call first.

"Mom!" I cried as she answered the phone with, "What?"

"*Mom*, I have the second-best Nextdoor.com post in the history of Nextdoor.com!" I exclaimed.

"If this is an internet porn thing, I'm hanging up right now and then hanging myself," she replied.

"No!" I answered. "I wrote a fake post on a social media site for neighbors, and my neighbors believed it and got all upset!"

"Why would you do that?" she asked.

"Because it's hilarious! I wrote that I wanted people to stop walking in front of my house because it makes Maeby bark."

"Why is that funny?" she asked. "I hate it when people walk in front of my house. Why can't they just drive like everyone else?"

"I know! And my post beat out the one by a lady who claimed that her neighborhood stroll was ruined because someone was using a Snuggle dryer sheet, which she insisted was going to give her cancer!"

"You live with kooky people," my mother said. "Snuggle never hurt anybody! What are your clothes supposed to smell like? *Nothing?* Nothing smells dirty. Snuggle proves that they are clean."

"I couldn't agree with you more," I said. "My post even beat out the third-place winner, which was an alert to the neighborhood that all of the avocados at Whole Foods were hard as rocks!"

There was a pause.

"That's not funny," she said. "That's something I would probably like to know."

"Well, anyway, I beat her," I said. "This is the best thing that's ever happened to me."

"Guess what happened to me?" she asked. "I got a package, and there was a wig inside of it. I didn't remember ordering a wig, but I said, 'What the hell,' and tried it on. It looks horrible on me! Now I don't know what to do with it or who it really belongs to, and Daddy already threw away the box because he can't wait to throw away a friggin' box. It's like that's his life's mission! Now how the hell do I find out whose hair is in my bathroom right now, shedding?"

"Mom," I said as calmly as I could, "can I call you back? I think I just figured out how to unseat Loud Boom on Buzzfeed next year."

Hiiiii Hooooooo!

I would be lying if I said that I wasn't flat-out terrified.

I pulled up to the building, parked, and took a deep breath. And then another one. And then another.

It felt like the first day of high school, when I'd been sure that the moment I walked through the school doors, some upperclassman was going to force me to do LSD, invite me to a fistfight, and then jump me into a gang. *Afterschool Specials*, though highly entertaining to me now, had such a chilling effect on me that I didn't make eye contact with anyone until my sophomore year and believed that anyone who offered me a piece of gum was a drug dealer trying to get me hooked on their "junk."

This time, although I was sure that no one in the building was peddling LSD or planned on beating me up at lunch, I had no idea what to expect once I entered. I had been under the impression that going gray meant settling into my life, slowly sinking into an imprint in my couch cushion, preoccupied with finding a good coupon for Ensure and communicating with the outside world mostly through Nextdoor posts.

I was about to start my first day of work, something I hadn't done since I walked out of the *Arizona Republic* newspaper doors for the last time in 2002.

Yes. I said "work." "Work" as in job. "Job" as in office. "Office" as in not wearing pajamas and pecking at a filthy keyboard with strawberry jam compromising the G, M, and 9 keys.

It had unfurled like this: My last book, a historical novel about three female aviatrixes that attempted the transatlantic crossing in 1927, was released the week that former FBI director James Comey notified Congress that the FBI had started looking into newly discovered emails.

I don't know if you remember that event and what happened afterward, but I do. I was on tour in Chicago that day, and by the time I got to New York the following week, my editor broke the news that the book was doing terribly. In fact, she said, all books were doing terribly, and book sales had come to an abrupt halt all across the board. It was simply a matter of timing, and in the publishing business, timing was everything.

She asked for the bill, plunked down her corporate card, and paid for the lunch that I had lost my appetite over, and I never saw her again.

You know the saying that you're only as good as your last movie? Well, the same applies in the book world. If your sales are great, you get a new book deal. If they aren't, you had better find a job. And fast. And when your hair has gone from brown to gray during that time, good luck finding gainful employment that doesn't involve a hairnet. The only positive thing about being thrown out of five community colleges and having a taste for liquor was that these factors delayed my college graduation for about a decade. To employers, that didn't put me at fifty, but forty, which meant that they had a better chance of hiring someone who would not die on the job or need a lot of sick leave for hernia surgeries.

To be honest, I had a great run as a stay-at-home writer. Many writers aren't that lucky, and I appreciated every minute of my time with the jam-encrusted keyboard. I considered trying to ride the downswing out, picking up freelance writing jobs here and there, but the year prior, my husband had been diagnosed with MS, and as the insurance carrier in our family, I started to feel like a steady job with benefits was a smart move.

Through the grapevine, I had heard about a temp position in the university communications department that was eight blocks from my house. I made a phone call and was shocked when I got a follow-up email asking if I could make a coffee shop meeting at 8:00 a.m. the next day.

On a regular morning, I wasn't even drinking my first cup of coffee at 8:00 a.m., let alone being showered, dressed, and ready to talk about a job. I wondered if there hadn't been a mistake. I didn't remember jobs starting so early, but when I responded that I would be there at 8:00 a.m., I didn't get a reply correcting me. So I showed up at the coffee shop in my least weird outfit, my portfolio tucked under my arm.

My potential new boss's name was Tobin. He was younger than I was, had thick hipster glasses—which gave me hope—and was patient as I flipped through my clips.

"You know we've met before," he said when I was done pitching my skill set.

Oh shit, I thought. *This is where my antics come back to haunt me.* I tried to remember where I might have seen him before. *Please don't be the guy I yelled at in Trader Joe's for reading every single yogurt label's ingredients and hogging access to the whole dairy case. Please don't be the guy I had several strong words for after he devoured popcorn at the movies like he was a bear at a dumpster. Please don't be the guy who parked so close to me that I had to climb in through the passenger side, compelling me to leave a note on his car that said, "Great job, FUCKFA," because the only piece of paper in my purse was oily in spots and would not accept the ink for the "CE."*

"I'm going to cover a whole lot of bases and just issue a blanket apology," I said.

"Don't be sorry. I only buy records at garage sales, but my girlfriend bought your *Sex and the City* book."

I blinked.

"You were at my garage sale?" I asked. "Oh, you were the guy who came with the two super-pretty girls?"

"My girlfriend and her sister," he said.

"Do you know that you're in my second-to-last book?" I asked. "I wrote about you! I feel so bad that she bought that book. I'd spilled Pepsi all over it."

"So the person you'll be filling in for went into early labor this morning. Can you start tomorrow?"

"What time?" I asked, hoping he'd suggest noon.

"Eight a.m.," he said.

"It's a deal."

I had a job. I was the temp.

Sitting in the parking lot and waiting for Tobin to arrive, I had no idea what to expect. The last time I had been in an office, I was this close to having security accompany me out, so I decided to just smile a lot.

Tobin took me around the office and introduced me to several new coworkers who seemed very nice. Then he showed me to my cubicle. I was looking forward to meeting more people and having a work lunch. The cubicles were arranged in rows, and once I started unpacking my things and taking a look around, it took me a minute to realize that I had not been shown to the area where I thought I should be sitting—the row with the hip, fit, thirtysomething writers. Instead, I was setting up my pencil holder in the quietest row in the office, and I couldn't help but notice that everyone in a two-desk radius had gray hair or no hair at all. I had been assigned to Death Row.

"Hey!" I wanted to scream to Tobin and anyone who could hear. "I wore Doc Martens the first time they were cool! I was the first punk rock kid at my school! I AM SITTING IN THE WRONG ROW!"

Instead I kept smiling. I held my tongue and thought about the insurance benefits.

After settling in, I properly introduced myself to Shar and Melody, my closest rowmates, who were very welcoming.

"We're all wearing red tomorrow to signify women's power in the workplace," Shar told me. "You should too!" I began to wonder if I'd been too quick to judge.

My gray-haired compatriots took me to lunch that day, and I stopped myself from ordering the fried food variety plate, instead mimicking their orders of salads to show them what an adult I was, which guaranteed that I was going to have to scavenge some more food for a second lunch in about an hour.

"We heard you're a writer," they said, and I nodded. Better lay all my cards on the table.

"I was, but I need insurance, so now I work with you!"

When we came back from lunch, Shar showed me her work space, which was decorated with lights, creepy little dolls, and personal photos. One of the photos showed a girl in Docs with deep black hair and thick black eyeliner. I thought it was me. Was this a joke? Had they dredged up something on Google and printed it out?

"Who's that?" I asked, pointing to my doppelgänger.

"Ha!" Shar laughed. "It's me. Right after a run in the mosh pit."

"No way," I replied. "Nineteen eighty-three?"

"Nineteen eighty-two. I already had my daughter by then!"

"That is badass, Shar," I said.

She giggled.

Melody's cubicle was just as awesome, decorated with black-and-white photos of her family and a gorgeous shot of a farmhouse overlooking a sprawling valley.

"I grew up there," Melody said. "My dad had a ranch. One hundred and forty acres."

"She was a barrel racer," Shar piped up.

"It's not like being in the rodeo!" Melody said humbly. "It was 4-H."

"I would bet that you're the only barrel racer in this room," I said. "That is also badass."

"I was also the first woman reporter in my town," she said with a twinkle in her eye.

"Duuuuuude," I said, forgetting that I was at work. "I love this row!"

"Oh, wait!" Melody and Shar said. "You have to meet Marlitt and Maggie!"

We crossed the office to the graphic design department, where my new coworkers introduced me to a few other ladies "our age."

"Marlitt designed Iron Maiden album covers," Melody said. "And this is Maggie."

I turned around and there was a woman with fire-engine-red hair wearing a vintage dress and Docs.

"Hi!" I said, ecstatic that the dress code of this new workplace might allow me to be myself.

Over the next few weeks I started to think that my new job was awesome. I wrote stories about professors and their fascinating research, as well as stories about students who were doing amazing things (one had completed two NASA internships before she was nineteen). And I made commercials that were broadcast during the Pac-12 Championships. My coworkers and I went out almost every day for friend lunches, and on Wednesdays at 3:00 p.m., I started holding a cheese-and-cracker happy hour at my desk.

A few months in, we started organizing lunch parties. I brought in pizza dough and made enough pies for everyone in the office. Marlitt and I decorated the breakroom for the holiday party, and eventually I was even trusted enough to be shown the secret breastfeeding room, cleverly disguised as a utility closet in the ladies' loo. It had a couch, a potted palm tree, and a tabletop Zen garden with a tiny rake.

"Sometimes, you just have to take a nap," I was informed with a wink.

After a couple of months, I was pretty confident that I had found my place in the office. My friends and I laughed during breaks, texted each other from our cubicles, and gave each other knowing glances during staff meetings.

Still, most of my friendships were with the older crowd. It was hard to break through to the younger set of coworkers. I tried my best to smile when they passed by my desk, but then I remembered that I was newly invisible. They weren't noticing my friendly overtures. If I'd wanted to, I could have started stealing other people's lunches or staying on my own floor when I had something unavoidable to undertake in the bathroom. But I didn't. I wanted to be here for a while, so I stayed nice and see-through. Then, during one of our daily editorial meetings, I couldn't take it anymore. I had an announcement to make to see if I was really there.

"I would just like to alert everyone who parks near the building," I said calmly, "that I just saw a hobo do a doody in the alley."

"Laurie," Tobin said, "this is not the meeting for that kind of talk."

"Oh my God," said Emily, a member of the younger set. "Where? Which alley?"

"This is a public service announcement for the safety and well-being of my coworkers, Tobin," I explained.

"I'm going to have to add to the List of Words Laurie Isn't Allowed to Say during Meetings," he warned me.

"I didn't say *poop*!" I argued. "I said *doody*. That isn't on the list!"

"It is now," Tobin informed me.

"Which alley?" Molly, another one of my younger coworkers, asked. "I don't want to come to work with crap on my shoes!"

"Molly!" Tobin interjected. "Language."

"That's not on my list." I shrugged.

"Please tell us where it is," Molly reiterated.

"Eleventh and Mill," I informed her. "Right behind the methadone clinic. That alley is being used as a public potty."

So far, the List of Words Laurie Isn't Allowed to Say during Meetings read:

- Fart
- Shit
- Booger
- Poop
- Asshole
- Bullshit
- Wad
- Snot
- + Doody

"Am I allowed to still say *crap*?" I wondered aloud.

"Add it," Tobin said firmly.

"I'm sorry," Molly mouthed to me. "But thank you."

"I'm never going down that alley again," Emily added.

I thought that was progress, right? At least they had noticed I was there, floating around in a gray mist of curls and saying foul words every now and then.

As summer turned into fall and my temp status was extended, I really got into the groove of things. I was paid every month, not once a year, like with book publishing. And I didn't have to chase down a payment, like with freelancing. I stopped worrying about making my mortgage payments. Working for yourself sounds fantastic, but it's hard. There were some things that I was really glad I didn't have to worry about anymore. Like the IRS. If you think I'm joking, ask any writer how many years behind they are on their taxes and what their installment plan is.

And I was back to being a reporter, which was awesome. I was covering a particularly fascinating story about Vanport, Oregon, a Black settlement that had been washed away by a flood in 1948. I forgot my notes at my desk one rainy night, and I had to race back into the office to get them. About two feet from the door, I felt myself slip on the slate tile in front of the building, and the next thing I knew, I was doing the splits, which is a very unnatural thing for me. I was positive that one of my legs had just cracked off and rolled into the street. I can't tell you exactly how I got up and hobbled back to my car, except that I was functioning on pure adrenaline. When I got home, my right knee had ballooned up like a rising ciabatta loaf. Within the hour, I was in the ER getting X-rays. Nothing was broken, but my knee was sprained, and I had deep tissue damage to the muscles all around it. In a day, my skin turned blue, then purple, then black. I went to work on crutches, and my coworkers brought me cookies.

As my friends stopped by my desk to see how I was doing, every single one mentioned that they had also slipped on that slate tile in the rain. As the daughter of a construction expert (my dad's work includes Sky Harbor Airport, the Maricopa County Jail, the Phoenix Public Library, and Arizona State University Downtown Phoenix), I know that slate tile belongs in Arizona but never in Oregon. Add water to slate and you've got yourself a Slip 'N Slide. It certainly has no business being in front of a building in a town where there is one season for summer and three seasons for mud.

Everyone in the office had fallen. Tobin. Shar. Melody. Marlitt. Maggie. Molly. Emily. I hopped up on my crutches and took a tally of the people in my office alone—one of about twenty offices in the building—who'd had a similar accident and found that thirty-two of my coworkers had slipped on that tile.

I knew that something had to be done. I typed a very firm but nicely worded email to the building manager informing her of what had happened and that I was expecting medical bills to arrive any day. I also let her know that she could personally witness my gymnastics routine clearly on the security camera, as it had taken place directly before the front doors. And that the tile needed to be removed before someone in this building hit their head on it.

She responded that no one had ever complained before, that the security cameras only pointed inward, and that I should not expect any compensation whatsoever. And the tile was staying.

In earlier years, I might have let this go. None of my coworkers seemed willing to take up the fight. But I am a different breed, and I had shed almost all of my fear coat. I was also at a point in my life when calling people out for their unfair behavior was not only clearly the right thing to do but also the only thing to do. I had seen it happen too many times. People act poorly because other people have let them act poorly, and they have been able to get away with it for a lifetime. There is no sense of consequence. So I called a lawyer who looked up the title of the building. I waited on the phone while she considered the situation, but after a long silence she said that she couldn't help me. I called another lawyer, and another lawyer, and another lawyer. Each of them dismissed the situation without much of an explanation. The last lawyer finally told me that no one in my tiny town was ever going to take the case. The owner of the building belonged to a prominent local family that had ties to pretty much every law firm around—and had the biggest public park in town named after them. Plus, the building's owner was a lawyer herself.

I was furious and injured, but I had no recourse. When the hospital bill came, even with my hard-won insurance coverage, I still owed more than two grand. That made me even more furious. So I harnessed the power of my Death Row membership and did what any old lady would do: I got nosy.

When I was finally off crutches but still quite bruised, I made my way to every office in our building—all four floors. Not surprisingly, most of the people I talked to had taken a spill on the tile outside. I left my email address and phone number at each of those offices in case anyone else suffered a fall.

The reports started rolling in. And every time I got another email or call, I emailed that manager who had shut my complaint down again and again and again until she responded. In every email, I repeated how dangerous slate tile was when wet, and I referred to my medical bills. I attached pictures of my leg on a weekly basis to show her how long it took me to heal, until the black faded back to purple, then blue, then green, then yellow. I sent her my X-rays. I emailed her until I knew she was as furious at seeing my pain-in-the-ass name in her in-box as I was at her when she told me that she was refusing to accept responsibility.

A year later, I had left central comms and my Golden Girl row of friends and moved on to working at a college in the university. I missed my friends, but we still sent each other texts and met up for lunches in which I consistently ordered the fried foods variety plate.

It was Melody who first forwarded the email: a company-wide announcement that the slate tile was being removed and replaced by concrete. With traction grooves.

I never got my medical bills covered, and my orthopedist ended up suing me for lack of payment. I held out hope that justice would prevail and that the building's owner would cough up what she was responsible for. When I finally paid the bills, I still hoped that there would be some kind of karmic justice. The following year, all of central comms moved onto campus, closer to my new job, and that building lost the lease from its largest tenant. To this day, that floor is still empty.

Sometimes it takes an invisible woman to get something done. The slate was gone, and though a lot of us had been hurt, I'd played a critical part in bringing that hazard to light. I'd reentered the workplace, held a job, and left the place slightly safer and wiser. It may have taken my entire tenure there to get all of my coworkers to see me, but leave it to an invisible woman to yell so loud when it counts that no force can drown her out.

Are You Serious?

I was as surprised as anybody to find out that I really liked going to work every day. For almost twenty years, I had holed up in my little office at home, writing day in and day out by myself. The differences between me and Ted Kaczynski were nominal, especially if you factor in the rate of our beard growth.

I now had work friends. People who wanted to meet me for happy hour. People who wanted to go to lunch with me. People who asked me if I wanted to grab a cup of coffee on our breaks. Even people who didn't sit in Death Row became my friends, once I showed them that old wasn't catching.

Sure, there had been some mishaps at my job, but nothing terrible. I'd told someone to punch me in the face at the next staff meeting after a miscommunication during an interview, but I was immediately informed that this was not funny and that I needed to apologize for encouraging violence. After I asked, "Are you serious?" and got an answer in the affirmative,

I bought a ten-dollar box of chocolates and left it on my victim's desk with an apologetic note. And then there was the time that I accidentally kissed my boss, but I don't need to get into that here.

I loved seeing people at work, and everyone was pretty cool as long as I wasn't telling them to harm me physically. One day, several of my coworkers invited me along to try out a new bagel place. Since I'm originally from New York, I scoffed until Jim, who was from New Jersey, said he had tried it already and it was great. George, the boss I'd accidentally kissed a week earlier, said that he could also vouch for the bagel place; he was from the East Coast and believed it was awesome.

All right, I agreed. *I'm in. I'll go.* Another coworker, Maggie, was also going with us. She, I found out, was the same age as me, and had lived in New York City during the early '80s, which was evident in her taste—almost identical to mine. She sported vintage sweaters, had bright red hair, and wore Docs to work. I had sensed that we could be friends when I'd started but hadn't quite sealed the deal, so I was happy that she was coming along too.

Since moving to Eugene in 2004, I hadn't made very many friends. I was working at home and didn't have kids. I initially joined groups and took classes to meet people, but this was an utter failure. It was hard to meet people when the most social experience I had was going to a doctor's office. Almost fifteen years later, I had three friends outside of work, and one of them actually was my doctor. But here at work, the potential was incredible.

So George, Jim, Maggie, and I ventured to the bagel place the next week, and I was happily surprised.

"This is a great bagel," I said, cream cheese lining my mouth. "This is awesome!"

"The lox is fantastic," Maggie said.

"Laurie, I heard you kissed George last week," Jim said.

"It was an accident," George said quickly.

"Thanks for coming by!" the owner of the bagel place said as he stopped by our table. "How is everything?"

We learned that he was also from New Jersey and had been in the restaurant business for decades. When he moved to Eugene, he'd noticed an obvious hole in the culinary offerings.

"You are seriously saving my life right now," I said. "These bagels are great!"

"You have cream cheese in your hair," Maggie whispered to me.

"Well, tell your friends!" the owner said. "It's been a little slow, so I need help getting the word out."

After he left, I stripped the cream cheese out of my hair, resisted the temptation to eat it, and then had a great idea.

"Do you know what we should do?" I said to my new friends. "We should have a bagel party at work. We can order a bunch of bagels, get cream cheese, and everyone can pitch in!"

"That sounds perfect!" Maggie said. "I'll help you plan it!"

And she did. Together, Maggie and I took the orders and collected the money. Jim then went to pick the bagels up.

The whole office came, about forty people. We had a blast. For an hour, we hung out, ate, and talked like old friends.

"I heard you kissed George," Melody, who was in Death Row with me, said.

"I heard that too," added Shar, my next-cube neighbor.

"Why did you kiss George?" Marlitt asked.

"I did not kiss George," I replied staunchly. "Well, I did kiss George, but it was not what you think."

I explained that it was an accident. It seemed like I wasn't going to be able to sweep that story under the office carpet. George and I had met for lunch to talk about a story I was working on. Afterward, I was heading back to the office, and George was continuing on to a meeting on campus.

I will admit here that I am lacking in workplace etiquette and sometimes forget where I am. I thanked George for his help and reflexively stretched my arms out for a hug.

I know. He was surprised, as was I, but it was too late. George is polite and nice, so he stretched his arms out too. Caught off guard by my own actions, I headed for my right, and George headed for his left, which was, it turns out, the same place. Quickly, I found my face in the crook of my boss's shoulder, my mouth pushed up against his ear. MY BOSS.

"Georgethisisawkward," I squeaked, and as we jumped back like we had just stuck a fork into an electrical socket,

I saw a long red streak along the side of his face that was the exact color of my lipstick.

"Oh my God," I said. "I'm so sorry, I'm so sorry!"

I pulled away. George looked like he had just found a dead body in the woods.

"No, no, no, it's okay," he said.

"But I dragged so much lipstick across your face that it looks like you slit your throat," I told him. "You'd better wash that off before you go to your meeting or go home."

"Really?" he said, trying to wipe it off with his hand.

"Oh, that's not going to do it," I said, shaking my head. "You're going to need soap. And a washcloth. I mean, you really need to get in there and scrub. Like inside your ear."

Poor George tried to get it off, but he wasn't making any progress.

"You really need a solvent," I said, wincing. "But at least we know that if there was ever an Awkward Hug contest, we would win."

"Poor George," Melody said when I finished explaining.

"Poor George," Maggie added.

"Poor George," Marlitt chimed in. "He didn't deserve that."

And then we all looked over at George, who was laughing with Jim and had what still looked like a sunburn on the left side of his face.

"That could take years to wear off," Marlitt noted.

The bagel party, fortunately, was a hit, and everyone agreed that we should do it again in a month's time. When several weeks had passed, I talked to Jim, who said he would be happy to pick up the bagels again. I sent an email to Maggie saying that we should do it again the following Wednesday. She didn't object, or even reply for that matter, so I told Jim that we were on and sent an email out to the entire office.

On Monday, I went from cube to cube to take everyone's orders.

But when I got to Maggie's cube, she just stood at her standing desk and didn't turn around.

"Hey, Maggie," I said. "Bagel time! What kind do you want? Lox again?"

But she made no indication that she had heard me, so I leaned over to see if she had earbuds in. She didn't.

"Hey, Maggie," I said a little bit louder. Nothing.

"*Maggie*," I said again, thinking that she was just really into her work.

"I heard you," she finally said as she slowly turned around.

"Okay," I said, a little freaked out. "What kind of bagel do you want?"

"I don't want any," she said and turned back toward her computer screen.

"What?!" I cried. "You have to have a bagel; you love them!"

Maggie shifted her weight from one leg to another and then turned toward me completely.

"You know," she said, "I don't want your stupid bagels."

"Are you serious?" I said to her expressionless face. "But it's Bagel Wednesday—"

"And I really don't appreciate you trying to derail my event."

I paused for a minute, trying to figure out what I had done.

"You have an event on Wednesday?" I asked.

"Yes," she said snippily. "It's Crafternoon."

"Oh," I said. "What is . . . Crafternoon?"

"The flyer has been up in the lunchroom all week," she said. "We are carving pumpkins and then having a contest."

"Okay," I said. "We can do Bagel Thursday instead."

With that, she turned around sharply and ended the conversation.

I got the hint. I walked back to my cube and sat there, dumbfounded.

I scooted my chair over to Shar's cube and raised my shoulders and said, "Crafternoon?"

"Yeah, I was going to tell you that I can't come to your bagel party," she said. "It's Maggie's event."

I scooted back to my own cube.

Crafternoon. *Cool*, I thought. *Let the crafting roll on.* I emailed everyone again immediately and moved the bagel party to Thursday. Later in the day, hoping that Maggie had simmered down, I went back to Maggie's desk.

"Bagel Wednesday is now Bagel Thursday, so Crafternoon is safe," I informed her with a smile.

She ignored me.

"Maggie," I started, "I think we had a miscommunication—"

She whipped her head around like an alligator.

"I do not appreciate you trying to take my day," she snapped. "Pumpkins don't happen at just any time of the year, Laurie. They happen once a year. ONCE. People look forward to this. It's an EVENT."

"I'm sorry, but I didn't know," I explained. "I really like you, and I would not do something intentionally to anger you."

"How are we supposed to decorate pumpkins with glitter if there is cream cheese around?" she demanded. "That is a toxic cross-contamination!"

"It's not a problem because I moved the bagel thing," I explained.

"Marlitt!" Maggie shouted across the room. "Are you coming to Crafternoon?"

"Of course," Marlitt replied.

"And Melody is coming, and Jennifer L., and Jennifer W.," she informed me. "I have a list of people who have RSVP'd."

"I would really like to forget about the bagel thing," I said. "I want to say that I am sorry and that I didn't mean to hurt your feelings. I would like to buy your bagel for Bagel Thursday to make up for the confusion I've caused."

She looked at me. I could see her thinking hard about her next move.

"Would you like to see the collection of ephemera that we use to Mod Podge the pumpkins?" she asked.

"Sure," I said, and she took me to a file cabinet that was stuffed with old magazines and graphics.

"I have some magazines from the '50s that I could add to that," I said, extending another peace offering. They'd cost me a fortune, but at that point, I didn't care. I would rather give her my vintage magazines than have her declare workplace war on me. I was just trying to be the nice girl.

"That would be cool." She nodded and smiled slightly.

"And I apologize for not being seasonally sensitive to the timing of your event," I said. I was learning office politics, and it seemed that, to truly belong in Death Row, I'd need to take any and all crafting opportunities seriously.

"Thank you," she acquiesced.

I even entertained the idea of really trying to mend fences by attending Crafternoon, but my intuition told me to stay away. The gift of the magazines was a safe play. There were clearly going to be knives there, and if there was going to be red smeared all over anyone, it had better be the same color as my lipstick.

Maggie and I never really became friends after that, despite my ongoing efforts. I complimented her pumpkin, but we never clicked back into place. I still smiled and said hi in the bathroom or in the breakroom, but things were strained.

One day, I realized that I hadn't seen Maggie in a long time. Her stuff was still there, but she wasn't. I figured that she was on vacation, but then on a subsequent day, her stuff disappeared too.

I went over to the drawer of ephemera and found it empty. Everything was gone, including my vintage magazines. There was no announcement, no goodbye email. It only made me like her more.

I scheduled a Bagel Wednesday that very same week.

I Said Drug Me Like
I'm Judy Garland

When my husband turned fifty years old five years after I had,
I wished him a happy birthday and delivered a prediction.

"I bet you're going to get a camera," I said as he sipped his
morning coffee.

"Do you think so?" he asked, raising his eyebrows.

"I know so. And a stranger is going to shove it right up
your ass."

I spoke from experience.

Five years ago, I was a fresh fifty, still dealing with the sting
of entering a new decade. I was experiencing a little eczema
flare-up on a finger—no big deal. My doctor, a sweet man
who shows his dogs competitively, walked into the examina-
tion room and pounced on me like I was a lamb and he a lion.

"Laurie!" he cried. "You're fifty!"

"You lost that bet, too, huh?" I replied.

"We need to get you scheduled for a colonoscopy!"

"No," I'd said simply.

"Yes," he'd replied, still smiling.

"No," I'd repeated.

"Yes," he'd volleyed.

"My finger looks like it has dandruff," I'd said. "That's all I need from you, thank you."

"We really need to get you in," my doctor said.

"Are you trying to fill a quota or something?" I asked. "My pharmacy had a contest in which the person who administered the most flu shots won a pork roast. I will *buy* you the pork roast if you let this slide."

"I can't," he'd told me. "This is fifty."

"I'll do it if you do it," I'd replied.

He'd laughed. "I'm only thirty-five."

"Here's the thing with your lot," I had explained. "You tend to leave out vital details. For example, I once went in for a uterine ultrasound. Cool. I get some cold jelly on my fat rolls, and then someone waves a wand, right? Wrong. Instead, the lady told me to assume the position and pulled out something that looked like a boom mike. No one told me that was going to happen when they said, 'You need a uterine ultrasound.' No one said to me, 'A strange lady is going to present you with what looks like a prop on the set of *Debbie Does Dallas* and is going to want to put it in the place where strangers aren't allowed to go.'"

"Why did you need a uterine ultrasound?" my doctor asked.

"I probably had eczema on this finger," I said.

And then, without one more word from me, he typed something into the computer and told me that IT WAS AN ORDER.

"I've heard it's not so bad," he said with a smile that was fifteen years away from anal penetration with a GoPro.

Not so bad. Now, I really, really like my doctor. But what men don't know is what men don't know. I'm sorry. It's true. I can't trust anybody who's never had someone come at them with an ultrasound-enabled dildo when they were expecting a smear of jelly. I can't trust anybody who's never had cramps seize them so badly that it feels like there's a lady boa constrictor inside who is also experiencing cramps. I can't trust anybody who hasn't had a boob pressed so flat that it's like the center of a plexiglass panini.

I'd like all men, my doctor included, to SHUT UP about it being *not so bad*. Can't the ladies catch a break? My husband has never had a testicle placed in between two plastic paddles that were cranked tighter and tighter and tighter until the testicle was as thin as prosciutto. You know how I know that hasn't happened? *Because we'd still be talking about it every single night.* Even if it had happened decades ago, we'd still be in therapy over it, because at the end of every sentence, he'd add, "And then my balls were squeezed so tight in a vise that I gave up on life and wanted to rip those balls off and dry heave in a corner."

"I know it's garbage night, but I'm going to wait until it's dark so that no one sees me in this T-shirt with a hole in the armpit. And one time my balls were squeezed so tight in a vise with a hand crank that I gave up on life and wanted to rip those balls off and dry heave in a corner."

"Either the dog farted or a portal to hell just opened up in this house. And one time my balls were squeezed so tight in a vise with a hand crank that I gave up on life and wanted to rip those balls off and dry heave in a corner."

"I'm a vegan, but I'm allowed to have meat three times a week on this diet. And one time my balls were squeezed so tight in a vise with a hand crank that I gave up on life and wanted to rip those balls off and dry heave in a corner."

Instead, because it was I who had the mammogram, I just had to complain quickly and move on with my life, but let me take this opportunity to correct that imbalance. It was and continues to be a truly awful experience. And you know what else is inhumane about mammograms?

They don't even let you sit down.

They don't even let you sit down.

You have to stand the whole time like you're waiting in line at Safeway to buy frozen chicken breasts and tater tots.

And then, if you're lucky, there's a bowl of mini candy when you drop your smock off. Like not even fun size. Smaller than that. The really small ones that are sort of square and sad. My mammogram place at least gets Hershey's, but honestly, after I drop my smock in the bin, I want to grab a handful of them, march to the lobby, and throw all of them at the receptionists, screaming, "FUCK YOU AND YOUR STUPID BABY CANDY! I WOULDN'T EVEN GIVE THIS SHIT OUT TO KIDS I DON'T KNOW ON HALLOWEEN. GET CLOSER, GET CLOSER, NOW LEAN IN. YOU JUST FLATTENED MY WHOLE TIT. GET CLOSER, GET CLOSER. GIVE ME A WHOLE FUCKING MILKY WAY FOR MY TROUBLE! DO YOU UNDERSTAND ME?"

So, yeah, dude. "Not so bad." Is that also how you'd describe my annual Pap, in which a lady I *do* know puts a freezing cold metal gun in my cooter, cranks it open like she's using a friggin' car jack, and then takes a swab and pokes it at my cervix like it's an arrow looking for the bull's-eye?

"Now just a pinch."

If someone pinched me like that at work, at the movies, or at a restaurant, they'd be leaving with a black eye, and I would be facedown on the floor with my hands behind me. The whole thing would be uploaded to Facebook in about thirty seconds.

Women get pinched, poked, pressed. Phallic symbols disguised as medical devices pop out of nowhere, and we just say,

"Okay. Fine. Come on in. Do what you want. I heard it isn't that bad."

I looked at my doctor (yes, I am still there in this story), and I said, "What's the prep?"

He cleared his throat. "Well, the gastroenterologist will prescribe a drink that assists you in clearing out the colon so that it is clean. I don't think it tastes very good, but I'm sure that you can doctor it up with something. They might have tips for you."

"That's not what I mean," I said. "I know about the drink. I mean *the prep*. This is something guys don't know. The prep. If I wear a dress, I know that I have to shave my legs. If I wear something sleeveless, I make sure that my armpits are freshly shorn. What, exactly, is the area prep in this situation? How involved does it need to be? I've never had an anal viewing before that I know of."

Because, really, it's no longer the '90s, when we could all get away with the swipe of a Bic razor while standing in a bathroom stall at the bar and call it good. And the guys from the '90s, God bless them, did not care what kind of overgrowth was going on behind the fence. They did not give a shit. They were just happy to be there. Even if there were red flags or possibly open sores, they trudged on ahead. We're the HPV generation, after all. I'm not afraid of no genital warts! Thirty years later, we've entered a wax era, and some overachieving women have ruined it for everyone else. They not only wax but also bleach, vajazzle, sculpt, and scent the musty places that were only meant to be explored in the dark. Even if I am a '90s woman at heart, the last thing I wanted to have on my anal record was a doctor's note that said, "Plain old butthole. Lack of attention to detail. This woman stopped caring decades ago. Probably homeless." I wanted to know what was expected of me and make an informed effort.

My doctor thought for a moment and actually delivered a great answer. "It's whatever you feel comfortable with."

And to me, that was great news. To be honest, I didn't want to prep. I didn't care if I was facedown and my gastroenterologist confused my anal region with an old Italian man's. I didn't care if he thought he had Andrew Cuomo on his table. If I had to go under the scope, I just wanted to get it over with as soon as possible.

Not long after, I was at the gastroenterologist's office, getting my prescription for the "drink."

"I'll be asleep, right?"

"Of course," they said.

"You'll wake up and it will all be over," they said.

"Will I be in pain?" I asked.

"Absolutely not," they said. "We are very careful and take every precaution."

I nodded, suspicious of people taking advantage of me while I was passed out cold. I mean, I knew what I used to do to friends who were blackout drunk when I was in my twenties. Unsuspecting friends would wake up with faces full of questionable makeup, or with foul things drawn on them in Sharpie marker. On one occasion, someone woke up with finger cots (think tiny little condoms) on every digit and didn't regain feeling in those areas for a week. Was it nice? No. Was it funny? It was hilarious.

I was pretty sure that twentysomethings would not be performing my colonoscopy, and I'd passed the age where I thought that vandalizing a passed-out friend was a great idea, mainly because I no longer bought my makeup at Safeway, and I had an arthritic hip that made it tough to move deadweight around. But still. I'd reached a stage in life where I didn't think it was so awesome to make a friend go to work and testify as a DNA expert at a murder trial with a handlebar mustache scrawled across her face in permanent ink.

There was every reason to be confident going under. But every now and then you hear about a medical professional taking pictures when they weren't supposed to, and I would be lying if I said that I wasn't terrified of a photo popping up on CNN that showed my butt growing carrots or several fine heads of broccoli.

There wasn't much I could do about the vulnerability. When I left the office with my script for the human equivalent of liquid plumber, I was on the books for a colonoscopy. *Honestly*, I told myself, *maybe my doctor is right. How bad could it be? I get to take a nap in the middle of the day! How often does that happen?*

The gastroenterologist does this nine to five, I reminded myself. *He probably sees eight to ten old, withering assholes a day, right? He's not going to remember yours! Plus, most likely, if there was something unusual, unique, or out of the ordinary about my asshole, someone surely would have said something about it by now. I would know!*

When the time came, I picked up the cleansing drink and steadied myself. Per the instructions, I couldn't eat anything but clear liquids the entire day, which was in itself rather traumatizing. I have never been so hungry in my life. I watched my coworkers eat lunch while I sipped chicken broth diluted with my own tears. When my husband took a bite of his vegan stir-fry, I almost knocked it out of his mouth and then licked it up off the floor.

I started the gallon of cleanse that night, and what I can tell you is that if you ever wanted someone to invent a cocktail made with salt water and Pledge, this is your drink. I was afraid to spill any of it as I gulped it down. I feared that it would eat its way through the old oak floor and make a skylight into our basement.

And it turns out, you cannot doctor it. You can add powdered Propel, stevia, Sweet'N Low, or simple syrup. But do that and you'll just end up making it even more disgusting. I promise. The best option is to hunker down and guzzle as much as you can take. Imagine that your family has been kidnapped by insurgents or pirates; your dog is being held for ransom, and this is the only way to get her back. Or imagine that someone has pictures of you with a broccoli farm growing out of your ass crack, and they will be sent to CNN unless you imbibe this foul fluid.

However, all was not lost. I was determined to beat the colonoscopy at its own game, so the day prior to the fast, I ate no solid food. Just smoothies, soups, and puddings. Ice cream, sorbet, and milkshakes. I was hoping that this would decrease my time in the bathroom the night before the event. And it did. I was only seated on the pot for an hour, as opposed to all night, which was a huge relief. But what an hour it was.

If someone had inserted a power washer into my GI tract, I do not believe that it would have been any cleaner. I was Roto-Rooted so thoroughly that I could barely remember my name afterward. Pieces of detritus from 1996 fell out like root balls. I said farewell to every aspect of my human self that wasn't necessary to stay alive, including some things I've probably paid for, like the residue of painkillers I've bought in a foreign country and a silver ring that's been missing since an alcohol-related blackout in 1992. Silver lining: in an hour, I lost ten pounds. You can't lose weight faster than that, even with an amputation.

My husband drove me to the appointment with a promise that I could stuff my big fat starving face with IHOP pancakes afterward. I'm sure that IHOP, the closest restaurant to the hospital, does great business with the post-colonoscopy crowd.

At the hospital, it took forever before I was actually prepped and ready to go. I had some questions for the woman administering the anesthesia.

"Does anyone wake up in the middle of this thing?" I asked.

She thought for a moment. "Sometimes. But it's very rare. It'll be over and done before you know it."

"Listen," I said with the bouffant cap on my head. "Drug me like I'm Judy Garland. I mean it."

"Oh," she said in a comforting tone, "we'll take good care of you."

"No, I'm serious," I insisted. "I'm going to need something stronger than a regular human dose. I'm from the '90s, and I take sleeping pills like they are Tic Tacs."

And that's the last thing I remember before I woke up in a movie theater, lying on my side, surrounded by people in masks and caps.

Maybe this is the new uniform at IHOP, I thought hopefully, but within several seconds, it was clear that I was in a room full of strangers who were watching a man play a video game maze that was all red tunnels. There was a camera, not just up my ass but way beyond that.

"Um, hi," I said to the audience, who suddenly turned their attention to me. "When I said, 'Drug me like I'm Judy Garland,' I really meant it."

This was way worse than carrots in my ass. It was like being one of the women in *Eyes Wide Shut*. I was the only one exposed in a room full of masked people. I didn't even want to imagine what was hanging out of me. I could only picture it as a plumbing snake, a coiled silver rope that you could buy by the foot at the Castle Megastore.

"Oh," the anesthesiologist said. "Do you want to go back under?"

"We're almost done," the doctor interjected. "Look! There's a pocket of diverticulitis right there on the left!"

"Is that what entrails are supposed to look like?" I asked. "Or am I one big gurgling mess?"

"You're looking good!" he said without missing a beat. "And you did a really good job prepping!"

I didn't know what to say to that. I did the best I could, but my razor was surely on the dull side.

My husband was waiting for me in recovery, and this is the second bit of golden advice I will pass on to you: After your colonoscopy, you will feel a very strong urge to pass gas. DO NOT DO IT. You must wait until you have pants on, because otherwise your jelly-lubricated fart will land on the floor, in front of your husband and the nurse, who will then have to bend down and clean it up.

My husband and I went to IHOP, and I have to hand it to the anesthesiologist, who finally got it right in the end, because I passed out right after my blueberry pancakes were delivered, my head on the table, exactly like Judy Garland.

Mother's Little Helper

"I haven't slept for three nights," my mother said as soon as she answered the phone. "I can't think. I can't sleep."

I already knew that whatever was bugging my mom was my fault. It's always my fault. It was my fault that she missed a sale on ham at Fry's last week, because, as she said, "I threw out my back picking up a piece of your hair in the bathroom. And I've never seen a price like that on Boar's Head before. I know it was a typo. They'll never go that low again. *What* did I tell you about your hair?"

My mother hates my hair. She actually hates all hair, particularly when it's not attached to a head, and can gag on cue if I just say, "Hai . . ." But she hates *my* hair especially because it's gray, and as we already established, she thinks that my gray hair makes her look old. The last time I stayed at her house, she said, "When you brush your hair, do it outside," and when

I walked outside with the comb, she yelled, "OVER ON THE GRASS!"

So when my mother said that she couldn't sleep, I already knew it was my fault. I steeled myself.

"Christmas is all ruined after what you did!"

What I did was have surgery. I had 65 percent of my stomach cut out in an attempt, yes, to lose weight, but mainly to kick the ass of the diabetes that had found a nice home in my pancreas. Well, I didn't lose the weight, but I am no longer diabetic, and all my mother cares about is that I can't eat what she's making for Christmas dinner, which is lasagna. Carbs. And that's bad. We're an Italian family, and food is as important to the holiday as a virgin giving birth to an illegitimate baby in a horse stall.

"You don't have to tell your doctor," my mother argued. "Two bites aren't going to kill you."

"I don't know, Mom, let me consider that," I said. "What do I like more, lasagna or my legs? Lasagna or my sight? Lasagna or my kidneys? What the hell! I'll take two pieces!"

"It's not Christmas if you can't eat Christmas food!" she cried. "I'm not even calling it Christmas anymore. We should just call it One More Stupid Day with Shitty Stupid Food!"

"Don't worry about it," I said. "I'll bring my own food. The beautiful thing about cottage cheese is that you can even buy it at a gas station."

"That's not going to be very appetizing for the rest of us," she countered. "No one's going to want to sit next to you."

"Then I'll eat it outside, on the grass," I replied. "And if you still can't sleep when I get there, I'll give you some of my Sonata."

"Oh," she said, "don't waste my time, Laurie. I have Ambien. Sonata is like Chiclets. But maybe if you bring the good ones?"

And this is when I deliver my holiday gift to you. As I mentioned, after I mocked a commercial for restless leg syndrome, I got it. And you can mock me and my restless legs—I don't give a shit—because after trying to deal with the effects on my own, I found out that the treatment for restless leg syndrome is a nice, tidy dose of Klonopin, a beautiful little orange tablet, every night. After I got my prescription, every night I got to drift away to sleep on a delicious benzo cloud. I always hope that it will carry me to the next day, but it typically deposits me back in reality within an hour. If Michael Jackson had done a little more research, he'd be in prison today and not a legend.

Last year, I made the mistake of giving my mother one of my orange tablets when she was nervous about going to the dentist. She had postponed three times due to anxiety, so naturally I wanted to help. She ended up going to the appointment, but she was so relaxed that she agreed with the dentist when he suggested that he pull all of her teeth and give her implants instead of a root canal.

Mom got new teeth. And I got a client.

I have become my mother's plug, her connection if you're from the '90s.

To be clear, my mother has two bad hips, arthritis, back pain from picking up my stray hair, and gamer's thumb from when she got addicted to Candy Crush. My mom is in discomfort most of the time, as even my father will tell you. Due to her gamer's thumb, she has to call him in from the other room to help her work the remote control.

"She's in a lot of pain," he told me not long ago. "I'm running downstairs every friggin' time *Jeopardy!* is over and the Duggars come on."

So when she asked for another pill, I figured, *Who am I to deny my mother a couple of comfortable hours?* Wasn't it in the spirit of the holiday to gift those we love what they long for?

On Christmas Eve, right when Santa was due to arrive, I found myself making the drop of an adorable orange tablet at the feet of the St. Francis statue on her nightstand. It was a milestone of sorts; years after she threatened to throw me into rehab in the early '90s because I was doing too much Tylenol PM, my mom and I were finally doing drugs together. It's sweet in a way. We finally have something in common.

And Christmas morning, when she was still sleeping on that benzo cloud, I tiptoed downstairs quietly, went into the bathroom, and brushed my hair in peace.

It All Goes Gray

It does. It all goes gray.

I mean, if you think about it, it makes sense. Everything ages; time does not freeze for any living thing. You are marched through the process, year after year, decade following decade, until, if you're lucky, you are at that moment when you cease to be, as thin-skinned, wrinkled, and vulnerable as a newborn. Flowers bud, blossom, and shrivel, and so do we. Young people don't understand that, simply because they haven't been alive long enough to see the process, and, most likely, we ourselves don't see it until we're far and obliviously past the bloom stage.

Young people see old people and believe that they were born that way. They don't know that the shrunken, hunchbacked woman at Safeway who asks for their help to reach a can of peaches was once a raging beauty who could outrun any boy. That the bald, freckled head of an elderly gentleman was once full and thick with reflective hair that was indistinguishable from the heads of the thousands of other young men who marched along-side him to war or crowded onto commuter trains with him.

We are not born old. We worked to get there. And it is such a surprise when you realize that your new body has been absorbed by a different one; freckles aren't where they used to be, and parts that were visible are now obstructed. It's a jarring moment, full of terror, anger, and wonder. It happens to every single one of us who stays alive long enough.

But no one sits down and has the Talk with you about how your body is changing, your hormones are dying like they're on a muddy battlefield in France in 1917, and you're about to enter a new phase of your life.

Honestly, I don't get it. Why give me the Talk when I was a child and had no idea what to do with that information but then stay silent as my body takes on the proportions of a melting candle when I could have been developing an informed, offensive plan?

My mother took on that first Talk when I was eleven, letting herself in and then closing the door behind her when I was taking a bath. She sat on the toilet and lit a cigarette. I don't remember much after that, just that something horrible had happened to me while I was sitting in tepid, filthy water, covering my little boobies with my hands as the water grew colder and colder. By the time she stubbed out the butt and left, I was a mess of misinformation, guilt, and bathwater filth. Let me put it this way: the biggest puzzle I was trying to solve at the time was that boys and girls were somehow different. I had two sisters, and we were very Catholic. There was no way in hell I had ever seen a wiener, and if I had, I'm sure my mother would have told me that it was a birth defect and to stop staring. "It's just a tiny extra leg in the wrong spot," she would have said.

I kinda feel the same way now—a little confused, a little angry, and, frankly, very surprised. As a culture, we prepare children for the next stage in their lives as they morph into adults, but where's the Talk about moving from an adult into an elder? It's honestly an even bigger transition, because I know for a fact that, when I was eleven, I didn't go to bed every night worrying that various aches and pains were cancer and that I'd be dead in a year. I want someone to stand in front of a room full of fiftysomethings with a filmstrip and a pointer to say, "This is where gas accumulates after a bean-and-cheese burrito. It feels like you are being stabbed repeatedly by a crazy guy on a bus who just snorted a pound of bath salts. But if you feel like an elephant is standing right here, that is a heart attack. If the pain is up here and it's burning, that is not a heart attack; it's because you ate a hush puppy three days ago and didn't sleep sitting up."

The thing is that, mentally, I don't feel any different than I did when I was twenty-seven and, to be honest, that was basically yesterday. I am still the same person. I still laugh at the same jokes, eat the same food, and like the same kind of movies. I am still Laurie. But now, every morning, I wake up and try not to pop a disk in my back just by getting out of bed.

I must be careful not to move my body other than as a unit, because I can now actually break it.

On Saturday, my friend Sara called. I didn't even get a chance to say hello before she shouted, "WHAT THE FUCK?!"

"What happened?" I asked.

"Dude," she said, trying to compose herself. "I was just at the store, okay, and my hair was up in a topknot, which some people might mistake as a little bun, and I was wearing a sundress, and maybe it was a muumuu—I guess it was a muumuu, I don't fucking know—but this guy came up to me after I loaded the groceries into the car and said, 'Ma'am, I'll take that cart for you.' And I was like, 'Fine. I really wanted to get my steps in, but here, take the cart if you need it,' and he took it and put it in the little cart roundup!"

"Oh my God," I said, wincing.

"LIKE I'M A GRANDMA," she continued. "Like I couldn't handle taking the cart back myself."

"Maybe he was a Mormon," I suggested. "You do live very close to a temple."

"The only thing that saved my self-respect is that, when I turned on the car, it was blasting Alice in Chains," she added.

"You do know that listening to 'Man in the Box' now sounds like when our parents listened to 'Rock Around the Clock,'" I told her.

"SHIT!" she screamed.

I totally got it. Only the day before, I was working on this very book when I heard a skateboard grind past my house. To clarify, I live on a hill, and my sidewalk that I've paid multiple times to repair is a hundred years old. It's cracked, broken, missing in places—it's a lawsuit waiting to happen. I do not have another fifteen thousand to fix it properly, and the city of Eugene still insists it's my responsibility. Awesome.

In five minutes, I heard that skateboard go by again, and this time I walked out to the front yard.

A teenage boy, maybe fifteen, sixteen, was coming up the hill with a skateboard under his arm.

"Do you not want me to skateboard down the sidewalk?" he yelled to me, and I could tell that it wasn't Owen, who lives on one side of my house, or Grant, who lives on the other. I didn't know this kid.

"Don't ride on my sidewalk," I told him, trying to stay cool. "Use the street; it's way safer."

And then, because his brain is not yet fully formed, he made a bad mistake.

"It's not your sidewalk," he informed me. "It's public property."

He must have been friends with the Nextdoor authorities. And then, because I still had the receipt from the time the city fined me for having a one-hundred-year-old sidewalk and forced me to spend a grand to fix it, I rose up onto my back legs like a deer and started rotating my hooves like a windmill of death.

"Bullshit," I told him. "If the city fines me to fix the sidewalk, it is my sidewalk." I was well prepared for this argument.

Instead of realizing the magnitude of his error, he told me to fuck off. I, of course, mimicked him, and he turned and walked up the hill to make another run.

So I shot back inside my house, grabbed a folding chair and the latest copy of the *New Yorker*, and sat myself right in the middle of the sidewalk for a standoff. He stood at the top of the hill, skateboard under his arms, and stared at me as I flipped through the *New Yorker* and pretended to laugh at the cartoons. Finally, he left, flipping me off as he rode away, calling me an "old bat." I pointed and laughed at him.

"Don't fuck with an old lady, you shitty kid," I yelled. "I have a lifetime of asshole tricks up my sleeve. They're all right behind my Kleenex and my emergency Advil."

Mind you, I was doing all this in no bra, sweatpants, and leather slippers with shearling lining.

"Sara," I asked, "when we all get together for dinner in a restaurant, do you think other people see a group of old people having dinner instead of—us?"

"Yeah," she said after she thought for a moment. "Yeah, I think they see old people."

And that's a trip, because when I look at Sara, I still see Sara. I see Sara as she was at twenty-seven. She hasn't changed to me.

Most of my friends haven't changed, in my opinion. Jim lost his hair, but so what? Lots of guys shave their heads. Sandra has a couple of gray hairs in her long, jet-black hair.

And yet, some of our friend group has died. From heart attacks. Pancreatitis. Liver failure. Drug overdoses. Suicides. Cancer. Aneurysms.

We were stunned by each of those deaths. Honestly, drug overdoses and suicides are almost easier to take than pancreatitis and heart attacks, because those diseases rarely happen to kids our age.

And then one day, your body stops working. It can be sudden, like throwing out your back while shaving your legs, and it just never goes back to normal. You live the rest of your days with a "bad back."

Then there's the opposite; there's the creep. In your thirties, a nerve pings in your hand, like someone has plucked a rubber band inside it. It's startling and odd. In another five years, your hands start to tingle a little bit when you're typing, and you buy a pair of hand braces to wear at night. In the next five years, you can't open a jar, and in the five years after that, they suddenly fall asleep and you have to elicit a hearty round of applause to no one to wake them back up and make them functional again.

And no one prepared me for that. I noticed that my nana's fingers were oddly formed, racked with arthritis, but she never explained that they hadn't always been like that. She never told me that once, a long time ago, she had hands just like mine, until she felt that first ping. And that's the weird thing. As a young person, you assume all old people were just always that way—unfortunate. They came like that. And, as an old person, you think that young people surely understand that yesterday, you were just like them.

My friend Laurie had a grandmother who did tell her things about aging, things that amazed and shocked her. When you tell a ten-year-old, "One day, I looked, and it was just a bald little monkey head down there," they are not going to get the whole story, but that mysterious sentence will be seared into their memory like it was administered with a branding iron. It will only make complete sense when they are fifty and look down and see that the monkey is starting to need Rogaine.

Maybe *AARP* magazine should have a centerfold to let us all know that when weird things start happening, like when my hair starts to get a little see-through on top, that's normal. And there's a special spray paint specifically made for that.

Amy texted me one day with a photo of herself, but there was something odd about it.

"WTF?" I texted back. "Is that a little bird in your neck?"

"Yep," she replied. "There is a vagina on my neck, and apparently things fit into it. And they stay. Without glue."

At first, I was relieved, thinking that she had gotten a tattoo I would have strongly advised against.

"You do not have a vagina on your neck," I texted back.

"I do," she said, and in the next photo there was an acorn where the bird had been.

Huh, I thought to myself. *If Amy has a vagina on her neck, I probably do too.*

I didn't even look; I just picked up a vintage rhinestone brooch off my desk and stuck it in the middle of my neck, around the spot where Amy had put her bird.

To my horror, it stayed. Two inches in diameter, and it stayed. Then I tried a pill bottle. It also stayed. And finally a tube of bloodred lipstick. It sucked at my neck like a bat.

"Amy," I texted back, "if you have a vagina on your neck, what the hell do I have on mine? I think I could pack a weekend's worth of clothes in there and still zip it up!"

Bald monkeys. Neck vaginas. These are things people need to know about before the day they just suddenly have them.

I know I have a vintage body, but I would like to have had a heads-up about things such as my lowest fat roll turning into a skin hammock almost overnight, even though I have never had kids.

My aforementioned friend Jim (now bald) actually loves the fact that he's almost sixty. He just opened his own recording studio after quitting a job that paid well but involved something called Oracle, which sounds ominous, in my opinion. If you have to consult an oracle as part of your job, there's no way you're getting paid enough; eventually a cyclops and a sorceress who can change you into a pig are going to show up in the breakroom, and, frankly, I have enough problems just trying to organize a bagel lunch. "I don't have to take anybody's shit anymore," he told me. Jim has also taken up carrying a cane just for the effect. He doesn't need it physically, except as a weapon. When he quit his Oracle job, he wrote a seventeen-page resignation letter with sections on each of his supervisors and coworkers and why he hated them. ("4. Jane, who sits behind me and eats tuna every friggin' day for lunch at her desk, chews like a horse and talks to her mother four times before the tuna sandwich happens.")

Jim loves his new life. One day he woke up and there were several wild parrots on a dead tree in his backyard. On Facebook, I watched the parrot numbers grow as he started to feed them, and he basically now has an aviary in his backyard. He spends most of his time out there feeding them and teaching them foul language. He's slid into his senior years with alarming ease. He even has a twenty-seven-year-old blonde girlfriend who wasn't quite yet born when we would tear through Phoenix drunk, stupid, and vomitous, so there's no skin hammock yet on his companion. He must be deliriously happy.

I suppose what I'm saying is that a little help visualizing my sunset years would have helped. By the time AARP invites started arriving, the ship was already taking on water. If someone would have told me about the equipment I'd need just to go to bed (hand braces, earplugs, pot gummies, face masks, heating pads, IcyHot, and a foot boot for plantar fasciitis) and that once I had everything on, looking like a hockey player, my husband would never be able to pick me out of a lineup, I could have worked on some shit when I still had some time.

Now it's too late. I'm here.

We're here.

And we're going to rock around the clock tonight.

It's My Menoparty and I'll Cry If I Want To

It had been almost a year with no word. Not a hint, not a nudge, not a stir.

At last, feeling confident that the change was complete, I bravely called my best friend. "Amy, I want a red velvet cake, bouquets of pink tampon flowers, and maxi pad streamers!"

"Oh my God, I'm so jealous!" she said. "I'll start making the guest list. It's going to be the social event of the year."

"It had better be," I almost shouted. "I've waited forty-two years for this!"

"I can't believe I'm going to plan my first menoparty!" Amy squealed. "I'm going to order dozens of red balloons days in advance so that they will be nice and deflated, like your uterus!"

It seemed too good to be true. But here I was, at fifty-four, heading down the home stretch of ovulation, ready to embrace my post-fertile life with glee and abandon. To be honest, I had been showing off for months, giving an exaggerated sad face to coworkers who entered my office in a panic, looking for a feminine hygiene product when they'd been caught frightfully unawares.

"I know that I look the same age as you, but to be honest, my uterus could make an appearance on *Antiques Roadshow*," I'd admit with an abundance of fake sorrow. "I don't even know if they still make tampons anymore; I'm so out of the loop."

When that coworker would leave to seek out another woman whose calcified bones weren't returning to their original state as a powdered mineral, I would get up quietly, close my office door, and laugh until my lungs filled up with acid reflux.

I don't care if that sounds callous. Since the age of twelve, I'd been attached to a maxi pad or a tampon, always having one within reach in case *that moment* came. I lived for more than four decades in abject terror, always afraid that a sneaker wave would hit, most likely on a date, during a job interview, or on a roller coaster, because a uterus cannot grasp the concept of inconsistent gravity. And I'm not the only one. Everyone who approaches the change of life has at least a handful of horror stories that would make Stephen King cry. I think the sheer dread of having another woman in their house was enough to make all Italian women encase their furniture with plastic covers in perpetuity on the off chance that a visitor might have a seismic eruption on a couch, because State Farm doesn't cover that, even though it would cough up some money if a man who was visiting sustained a bullet wound on some upholstery.

I, for one, loathed my cycles. There is absolutely nothing to celebrate there. My ovaries owe me approximately a dozen sheet sets, three mattress pads, assorted jeans, shorts, and so many pairs of underwear that I finally just started wearing black ones like all of the male characters in *Saturday Night Fever*, including the priest and probably Mrs. Manero.

The generations that follow mine apparently love to talk about their periods, or maybe it just seems that way. I blame the Kotex marketing team, who, after printing a bloodred dot on their packaging, broadly proclaimed that "there's power in sharing openly about all things period."

They're not the only one—Tampax now claims that its mission "is to make period conversations as normal as periods so women and all who bleed can feel educated, empowered, and limitless every day of the month."

And that, my friends, is bullshit. I want to hear about your period about as much as you want to hear about mine. Amy Schumer, with her Tampax spokesperson deal, can play with tampons and strings as long as she's getting a paycheck, because it's about moving product, not about empowerment, and not about having to insert a dry cotton cork every twenty-eight days.

Let's get this straight: My experience with menses was never walking hand in hand through a daisy field. It was more like a joust. Every month, she tried to kill me with pain, leg cramps, and the very real possibility of humiliation. I might wake up in a pool of blood, like there was a horse head looking at me. I tried to kill her with copious amounts of Advil, Midol, heating pads, and special period-time bike shorts that fit like a black condom and prevented the futon in between my legs from shifting. Anything that requires "extra leak protection" is not your friend.

If Tampax and Kotex really cared about period power, they'd invest in a little something called suspended animation. If you actually want to help while my ovaries, month after month, shoot out a stupid little egg that bloats me, cramps me, and makes me throw away DKNY sheets that I just scored at TJ Maxx for $39.99, put my ovaries in a friggin' coma and watch me go. Invest in *that* technology instead of braiding a tampon tail to help with leak protection. A flower print on a maxi pad or a fresh scent will never empower someone who has cramps that register on the Richter scale. But figure out a way to drug my reproductive organs into a stupor, and you've just introduced gas to a butane lighter.

And while we're at it, do me a favor and go back to using blue liquid in commercials when demonstrating a pad's absorbency. Using cherry-colored liquid isn't accomplishing anything except ruining Hawaiian Punch for all of us who haven't gotten cancer from drinking it yet.

I've found that the real empowerment comes from menopause, not periods. There were white sheets in my future, and I could finally buy a nice pair of underwear. Of course, my blap (belly plus lap) would cover most of the pretty parts. But who cares? I was delighted to trade my monthly ventures into womanly hell for a flesh canopy. The freedom I was about to embrace was priceless. I could spend the night as a guest at someone else's house without anxiously checking the bed in the morning. I wouldn't have to carry a handbag big enough to run away from Nazis with the family silver. And I could finally break up with my heating pad, a moment I couldn't wait for.

Menopause, however, is a fickle temptress. She will lull you for months with the absence of the curse. You will get used to a life without blood spill. You will no longer force a smile during staff meetings while cramps squeeze your lady parts like a python. Every month that Flo ghosts you, it is pure elation. It feels like glory. It feels like you've just done something magnificent. It feels like being eleven.

Now, I am not saying that traveling through the land of menopause is akin to stumbling upon a sample sale stocked with nothing but plus sizes; there are pitfalls. Take, for instance, the night I was at a library fundraiser and authors were rotating from table to table to talk to the guests about books and writing. I landed at my fifth stop and was three minutes into our chat when it struck: the inevitable hot flash.

Within an instant, and I mean *an instant*, my body reacted like a mobile home in which a tweaker had just set off a firecracker.

BOOM! My pores went off like an overeager sprinkler system, and beads of sweat rolled down the sides of my face. My hair was suddenly plastered to my head like that of the little girl in *The Ring*. The guests who were there to hear me speak stared unabashedly, some with their mouths hanging open. I was not surprised. It's not every day that you watch a woman literally melt in front of you. I excused myself and ran pathetically down the hall, searching for a bathroom, my body heat wilting the leaves of potted plants and blistering the paint on the walls in my wake.

It was my Fukushima of menopause.

I found the bathroom and flew into a stall, trying desperately to sop up the tidal wave of sweat with toilet paper, much of which stuck to my face in patches of cheap single ply. My dress was soaked in all of the bad places and would now require dry cleaning. If I'd farted, I probably would have seen a poof of ash.

So when it looks like your time has finally come, you hold on tight for months: Will she or won't she return? What are the chances? You eye the box of tampons, the stack of pads under the sink. You fantasize about what you can store in their place—jars of moisturizers for crepey skin, bottles of stool softener. Every new eye cream that comes on the market.

And then, just after your best friend starts pricing hundreds of red balloons, why, there she is again.

I have to be honest: sitting there in the bathroom, my stained white briefs sagging around my legs—ruined because I had been so brazen, so sure of myself—I felt a wave of grief covering me completely. It was the cruelest trick that Mother Nature—who must herself be so postmenopausal, she has to eat the actual bones of the young to keep her calcium level up—could ever play, aside from delivering a UTI and a yeast infection at the same time.

I was so upset that I actually made an appointment with my gynecologist. I had heard of a magical test that could tell you precisely where you were in the menopausal process. And that was huge, because if there's one thing I can only handle once a year, it's presenting my genitals to the Lady, who makes four hundred dollars every time she puts something in my cookie. I do it; I always make sure that I reply when they send the reminder postcard. But after managing to get my feet into stirrups forty-plus times, an act equivalent to planting the soles of both feet onto the sideview mirrors of a car, I really only prefer to go when summoned. I feel the same way about my Prius. Scheduling an extra trip to the dealership would require either a weird knocking sound or something falling off that I can't figure out how to put back on myself, even with the guidance of a YouTube video.

Now, to be perfectly frank, I'm at an age where not only am I not as flexible as I used to be, but there is also more real estate to relocate before the stirrups are even possible. The last time I went to see the Lady, I was in the position roughly twenty seconds before I was struck by a charley horse in both thighs. I'm like a Barbie now; my joints just don't *go* that way anymore. Forcing the issue is likely to have the same results as a rotisserie chicken asked to do the same thing. Chances are good to likely that all the inner strings keeping it together have either disintegrated or will snap back and hit you in the eye if you get too ambitious.

I explained this, and the Lady nodded with understanding. With my legs just far enough apart to put pants on, I tried to scoot down as much as I could, but it was hopeless. I basically laid on my back and let her fumble around my private parts like a sixteen-year-old boy. Then came the steel bear trap, the bite they take from your cervix, and we were done.

I cleared my throat. "I heard about this test," I started. "It tells you how far along you are in menopause. Am I making this up or do you know what I'm talking about?"

"Oh," she said with a slightly sad face. "I do know about that test, but it might not be too late for you. There are methods and things we can try."

I was confused. "Try . . . for what?"

"Well, if you wanted to take this last opportunity to get pregnant," she said.

Had I not been still clenching because of the indignity of it all, I would have pissed myself laughing. All I could think of was blowing into one of Amy's deflated red balloons, trying to bring it back to life.

"That is pure insanity," I told her. "If I can't reach down to tie my own shoes, there's no way I'm lying on the floor to tie my baby's booties. I'd have to hire a nanny just to help me get back up again. Plus, I want to retire someday and not work into my eighties to pay for someone's college education."

"I'm so glad to hear that!" she said, leading me to believe that the pinch I'd felt had been her pinning a DANGER! CONDEMNED! sign to my uterus.

I smiled. "Can we do the test? I'd like to know how close I am."

"Of course," she said, then sent me down the hall to get blood drawn.

I was finally going to have confirmation, and I was thrilled. I envisioned my red velvet cake in the shape of a uterus with Twizzlers for fallopian tubes and an icing banner screaming, "OUT OF BUSINESS SALE! EVERYTHING MUST GO!"

I started mentally creating the guest list, mostly focusing on people I knew would be jealous. I thought of games we could play: dunking for eggs, all dyed red; testing which incontinent pads really did capture the most lemonade; and playing "pill bingo," in which supplements, high blood pressure meds, and statins would be boxes on a bingo card, and you'd fill in the ones you had in your purse. Prizes would include compression socks, bottles of glucosamine, and packages of white underwear.

It was going to be awesome.

The next week, I received a letter in the mail from the Lady's office. I ripped it open like it was a tax refund, getting ready to hit "buy" on a light-pink bra and panty set that was still lingering on my computer screen.

One look at the results and I almost dropped the letter.

I wasn't in menopause.

That piece of shit letter told me, without an apology or a bouquet of flowers, that I wasn't even close.

I wasn't even in perimenopause yet. I was still functioning at full throttle.

"This is bullshit!" I screamed. Either my eggs were stuck to my ovaries with the tar I had collected from smoking, or I needed to call Georgia's secretary of state to demand a recount.

"MY EGGS ARE DEAD!" I yelled as I marched around the house, Hulk mad and knocking soft things over. "MY EGGS HAVE BEEN DEAD FOR YEARS! DO I HAVE TO STICK A TAILPIPE UP THERE TO FINISH THE JOB MYSELF?"

I got that letter last year. I still have not gotten over it, but I also still haven't gotten my period either.

And though I am convinced that I am indeed postmenopausal (for fuck's sake, I shoplifted potatoes and did not feel bad about it), Amy never ordered the balloons, and I am still wearing black underwear. Because Mother Nature is a bitch. And I wish I could put a curse on her, but if I did, I'm convinced that she'd rewind my reproductive system all the way back to eleven.

What Do You Mean She Doesn't Have a Pulse?

I had never taken a $250 car ride before, but there I was in Atlantic City, a place that, to be honest, was not on my bucket list.

It had just cost me a fortune to get there from the Philadelphia airport. My stomach twisted with horror as I handed my debit card to the driver, who was nice and all but had just made a quick fortune off me. I was determined to find a cheaper way back to Philly in two days.

A nonprofit had asked me to be the keynote speaker for a fundraising event called "Lunch and Laughter" that was being held at a fancy hotel with a hefty price tag, indicating that this wasn't my usual gig. These were actual ladies and not girls, and that was a little unnerving. I was certain that they had actually wanted Tig Notaro, and thought they'd gotten her for a steal. I was about to correct them, but then I thought, *Really, what's the worst that can happen?* I get up, bomb for forty-five minutes, come home, and buy a new smart TV with the check.

The audience consisted of 250 women from what I'd learned was a conservative-leaning area. I started to doubt that they'd been courting Tig Notaro, and I felt like even I needed to scrub up my image a bit. I searched through my cleanest material, looking for stories that were not likely to offend, and got to a place that I thought was sanitary but still packed a good punch line or two. It was time to (gulp) act my age.

But the morning of the luncheon, I sat in my hotel room and started to freak out. Certainly, someone from the organization knew who I was, right? I mean, my name wasn't drawn out of a hat. They'd called me. Surely, they knew that my books weren't spick-and-span clean. Surely they knew my topics and that I tend to say some "odd" things every now and then, right? Right?

I called my friend Amy an hour before the event.

"What if I just flop?" I asked her, feeling the onset of a panic attack beginning to form. "I mean, this is not like a reading on a book tour. These women paid for their lunches, and it's a fundraiser. I'm sure it was expensive."

Amy tried to reassure me. "The organizers had to have read your stuff before even considering you," she said, trying to calm me down. "Everything is going to be fine. Don't talk about VD or the DEA raiding your house in the '80s. Don't say that you dated a drug dealer. If you stay away from those areas, it's going to be great."

"What if I get booed off stage?" I asked her. "That happened once in Eugene at another fundraiser when I mimicked my Italian teacher having cramps during a date. No one was concerned that a college professor was dating a student, but substitute the *r* in *cramps* with an *l* and it's the crime of the century."

"Don't tell that story," Amy said quickly. "Are you going to tell the Disneyland story? I bet that would work."

"No," I replied. "The punch line in that piece is that I fell down on Tom Sawyer Island after getting soaked on Splash Mountain, and those rotten kids mocked me because I had big brown dirt circles on my boobs."

"Yeah, don't tell that story," she advised. "The time you tried to buy a little boy on the street?"

"No," I said sadly. "It's a satire of white privilege. I don't think it would go over well at a tea party, which this literally is."

"Getting booed off stage isn't the worst," she finally said. "It will make good material for the next book."

"I guess you're right," I said. "That would make a really good piece. I've never been heckled by a society matron, drunk on Earl Grey and nibbling on a cucumber sandwich before."

"See?" Amy said. "Either way it's going to be fine, if you rock it or bomb it. All comes out in the wash. But I am going to light a candle for you right now."

"Do you know that the trip down here from Philly cost me two hundred and fifty dollars?" I asked.

"Did that include lunch?" she asked. "You must have passed a million Philly cheesesteak places!"

"No, it did not," I shot back. "In fact, that was my whole budget for the trip. I can't afford the room service at this hotel, I have no car, and the closest restaurant is at a golf course a mile away. I've been eating out of vending machines and my purse."

"Thank God you always travel with Pop-Tarts," she said before hanging up.

I put the finishing touches on my makeup, ironed my dress, and went over my material one more time. When I had summoned enough courage, I found my way down to the ballroom of the hotel and was shocked at what I saw: a room full of women in fancy hats and full cocktail attire. One lady was wearing a sequined dress.

My clean stuff was not going to be clean enough, but it was too late. I tried to calm down and rewrite some jokes on the fly. After meeting with the board members and making sure one last time that they didn't think I was a lesbian with breast cancer, I felt a little better. They were nice and warm, assuring me that they had read my books and just wanted the ladies to laugh.

The lunch started, and after opening remarks, I was called up to the stage to do my set. I launched into my first piece, and right away it was going poorly. The women just stared at me, a lady with gray hair and cowboy boots, trying to sell them on why I thought that my cat taking a shit on my husband's pillowcase was funny.

I thought she was going to talk about breast cancer, I'm sure one of them was thinking.

I was struggling. And then it got worse.

Cue the flop sweat. My mouth dried up because every ounce of liquid in my body was flooding out on my forehead, in my armpits, and under my boobs. I wanted to throw up. Bombing does not just suck; it is painful. If you don't have the right material for the right audience, you'd rather be stabbed repeatedly than stay up there in front of a microphone. I stopped making eye contact with them and just read my piece. No matter how careful I had been, it was very clear that I had not picked the right material. This plane was going down. *Why weren't they serving martinis at this thing?* A loose audience is a great audience, but this crowd was wound up tighter than the Spanx around my left leg, which is marginally bigger than my right. I was waiting for a tea cake to hit me in the face, followed by a hook ripping me offstage, when it happened.

I got a laugh.

Then I got another. I heard a giggle. Then another laugh. Soon, more people were joining in. Things were picking up, and I fell into a rhythm. The audience was holding steady, and I was able to make eye contact again. It was such a relief, and I was feeling confident that on my next big punch line, the crowd would be mine. I ran, did the triple axel somersault of comedy, and stuck the perfect—and I mean *perfect*—landing, ready for peals of laughter and the adrenaline that goes along with it.

But instead there was silence. Not a sound. I kept reading and told another good joke, but the room grew even quieter. I couldn't figure it out. Nothing major had changed in the story. I hadn't veered into something suddenly political or particularly polarizing. My blood pressure plummeted, and the flop sweat was about to swallow me. Finally, I had to look up and see if there was any hope for recovery. But when I stole a furtive glance at the room, I saw that there was a crowd of women gathered at a table in the second row. There was a lady on the floor with another woman hovering on top of her, pushing on her chest.

"She has no pulse!" someone screamed.

A gasp went up. A woman had just died in front of me and 249 other women in fancy hats; I had no idea what to do.

"Someone call nine-one-one," I said into the microphone and, as seen on TV, asked, "Is there a doctor in the house?"

"We're nurses!" someone yelled, and I realized that the voice came from the collection of women who'd already gathered around the lady on the floor.

Now, I hate to make this about me, but if anyone reading this has ever had someone die in the middle of their punch line,

I'd like to know how you reacted. I had never killed anyone with a joke before, although I think I came close once during a reading in North Carolina. Several people in the audience had looked unconscious, and I'd started to worry about a gas leak. That time, it had turned out that a group had wandered over from a nearby assisted-living facility. At every reading at that bookstore, there were attendees who sat down and promptly fell asleep, appearing to have died. So that had been bad enough, right? Someone falling asleep during your performance is not a vote of confidence, but dying is something else entirely.

How many times can you say, "Can someone call nine-one-one?" "Has anyone called nine-one-one?" and "If no one has yet called nine-one-one, it would be a good idea to do that now," into a microphone? I seriously didn't know what else to do. Was I supposed to stand there onstage and keep calm? There was nothing but appalling silence as the nurses continued to perform CPR. The rest of the room was as frozen as the bunch of women who dared to glance back at Sodom and Gomorrah.

Tell me, Tig Notaro, what would you have done? I silently slunk offstage; found a nice, inconspicuous spot along the ballroom wall; and stood there as the paramedics ran in, took over from the nurses, and rolled the woman onto a stretcher.

One of the organizers came over, whispering, "She had an allergic reaction and choked on what might have been a mini éclair."

"That's terrible," I said. "I had to give my best friend the Heimlich maneuver once at a party when she choked on a mini quiche. Very similar circumstances, except that my friend was in a wheelchair dressed up as Blanche Hudson—I was Baby Jane—and she kept rolling away from me as I tried to Heimlich her. Really similar. Very similar. Terrible. My friend was also very drunk, and the Heimlich really didn't dislodge the quiche—she ended up swallowing it but then vomited it all up in my bathroom. There was a lot of vodka involved." I couldn't stop. I felt that I needed to fill the silence. "She was going through a divorce. Bad time. Her husband was a doctor who was cheating on her with his nurses. Got one pregnant. Well, not really a full-fledged nurse, not like those heroes over there, but you know, the person who checks you in. Their baby was very ugly. Homely little thing. You know how sometimes babies come out looking not done in the middle, or like a shrunken old person? Benjamin Buttonish? Well, this baby—"

"Look, she's sitting up!" the organizer interrupted as she swiftly walked toward the woman on the stretcher, who was now alive again and being wheeled out to the ambulance.

I thought about initiating a round of applause for the first responders, but the entire room was in a state of shock.

I think it's fair to say that none of us knew what to do. No one really wanted to go back to their tiny desserts and mini sandwiches. What had been a fancy Atlantic City fundraiser was now a room full of people who had watched someone actually die and then be brought back to life. If they weren't sober already, this was enough to knock out any chance of revelry. There was no chatter, no sign of relief—only cold, icy silence.

After a few silent minutes, the organizer made her way back to me with a smile on her face that told me something unthinkable was about to happen.

"Would you mind finishing up the last twenty minutes?" she asked brightly, as if she was not asking me to continue with a comedy set after we had just seen a woman resurrected. "The lady who died is going to be fine."

"Of course," I said, returning the smile, and clambered back onstage without an intro.

No one, and I mean no one, wanted to see my mouth behind that microphone again. And it took everything I had not to make a single Jesus reference, or comment that we should have had the resurrected lady change the tea into wine before she was wheeled off to the hospital.

But I finished my set. I got up there and I did another twenty minutes as if I were performing at a wake, which I guess, in a way, I was. It was twenty minutes that felt like twenty days, but at least this time around, no one died, choked, or had a seizure—or fell asleep, for that matter.

We were all far too alive to let that happen.

The next morning, I called a taxi service to book my return car ride to the Philly airport. The same guy picked me up, in the same car.

"How was your show?" he asked.

"I don't think it could have gone worse," I said.

"That's too bad," he said.

"Speaking of bad," I replied, "is this ride going to cost me two hundred and fifty bucks again?"

On the way into the city, he agreed to throw in his favorite cheesesteak, and while we drove there, he showed me the Liberty Bell and the steps that Rocky ran up and down. I wasn't particularly impressed, mainly because I had just seen a lady die and then undie. Even the Liberty Bell pales in comparison to that.

I decided to save my sandwich until I got on the plane, and I watched him carefully as he ate his one bite at a time in the car. Taking a bite. Swallowing without incident. Finally, when he was done and had tossed the crumpled wrapper into the bag, I took a breath. I stopped watching him.

"A lady died during my show," I suddenly blurted out.

"No shit," he replied.

"No shit," I answered.

"What'd you do?" he asked.

"I told people to call nine-one-one," I said. "I didn't know what else to do."

"Hmm," he said, nodding. "Seems like the only thing you could do."

"She came back to life, but it was still a drag for everyone," I added.

"Like Jesus?" he asked.

"Kind of," I said. "Except no one was very happy about that. They didn't even finish their desserts."

"Not much you can do after Death comes to a party," he told me.

"That's what I thought!" I agreed. "But they made me get back up there to finish my set."

"No shit," he said.

"No shit," I agreed.

"You get any laughs after that?" the cab driver asked.

"It took a while," I said. "But I got a couple."

"That is badass," he told me, looking in the rearview mirror at me. "No amateur could do that. That sort of shit takes a pro."

I thought for a moment. What would I have done if that had happened on my first book tour, when I was in my early thirties? What would I have done if that had happened on my second, third, or fourth book tour, well into my forties? I knew the answer. I would have had a panic attack if someone had asked me to get back on that stage. I doubted that I would have been able to do it. But by now, I had handled fifty-plus years of life. I had handled the deaths of friends and loved ones. I had handled getting fired multiple times; moving across the country to a town where I knew no one; watching my writing career explode; having my agent ditch me; being told that my husband was going to die in three weeks; going back into the workforce in my fifties; almost bleeding to death; and, most horrifying of all, waking up naked with something up my butt in a room full of strangers.

Life's greatest hits.

Now I had a new one.

"You know what you did?" the cab driver said.

I shook my head. "I have no idea," I chortled.

"You bitch-slapped Death," he said. "Death came to your party, and you threw that fucker right back out. Not here, not today, Death. You said, 'I'm going to make these people laugh no matter what you throw at me,' right? Isn't that right?"

I smiled, and I laughed for real this time. "I think that's right," I agreed.

"You know how many people can do that?" he asked. "I only know of one. Only one. And she's hanging on to that cheesesteak sandwich like it's going to be her last meal. You should eat that damn thing."

I smiled and unwrapped the sandwich, still somewhat warm, and took my first bite as the driver left Philadelphia and got on the freeway toward the airport.

He had eaten his lunch. We had even laughed a little. And he had survived. He was alive. I was going to recover too. It was one thing to finish a comedy set after a death, but hitchhiking the rest of the way to the airport was no laughing matter.

Take All of Me

"Are you sure you're feeling all right?" my endocrinologist asked, looking at me with a great deal of concern on her face.

"Yep," I said, nodding. "I'm totally fine."

"Except you're not," she said, furrowing her brow. "Your blood sugar levels are . . . high."

"Well, I know that," I said, having been diagnosed as diabetic several years before. "How high are they?"

"Your A1C is at an eight," she said, looking at me closely. "You really should be in a coma."

"I wish! I could use a good nap!" I laughed, but she didn't laugh back.

"I'm serious," she said. "By all medical standards, you shouldn't even be conscious."

And then I realized that she wasn't joking.

But I really did feel fine. I felt like I always do. Nothing different or out of the ordinary. I was just thirsty.

"Laurie, we need to bring this down fast," she said. "You could have sustained irreparable damage to your kidneys and eyes."

I also did not find that funny. But it wasn't like I didn't see this day coming. I had been diagnosed with polycystic ovary syndrome (PCOS) in my early thirties, when most doctors didn't even know it existed. Symptoms include sudden weight gain (check), irregular periods (check), chin hair (check), high triglyceride levels (check), and, the kicker, insulin resistance (check, check, check).

For more than twenty years, I had kept everything in balance with meds, staying away from carbs when they weren't calling me like a siren, until I hit fifty. And became diabetic.

At that point, my gynecologist took me off birth control pills, and things spun out of control like a basket of spiral fries at the fair. My great endocrinologist left, replaced by one who "didn't know much about" PCOS, so I offered to google it for her. Eventually, after changing meds four times and gaining another forty pounds, I fired her and found a PCOS specialist a couple of hours away.

My new doctor, Dr. Curosh, was determined to rein my diabetes in, but my biggest concern was that I couldn't fit into any of my clothes. I had just started my job at the university and was very self-conscious about my appearance. It sucked.

When you have PCOS, once the weight is on, it's like building an addition to your house—it's basically there forever.

And even more so if you're on insulin, which I now was, and a lot of it. Weight clings to you like a baby chimp clutching its mother. But even the insulin wasn't bringing my blood sugar down, so I was very overweight and also putting my inner organs in danger without even eating a Twinkie.

After I'd been seeing Dr. Curosh for about a year, I decided that I wanted to start taking appetite suppressants or fat pills like I'd seen advertised on TV. I went into my appointment determined to secure a prescription for something that would solve both the weight and the blood sugar disasters.

Dr. Curosh was very kind in her denial of my request.

"I'm sorry," she said. "Appetite suppressants are dangerous, and given what you have going on, losing weight is just not going to happen for you. We need to focus on getting your numbers down."

I was frustrated. "I can't take this anymore," I confessed. "There must be something I can do to get rid of this weight."

"Your metabolism is very slow," Dr. Curosh said gently.

"So I'm never going to lose it?" I asked.

"Probably not," she said.

"What if I was in a North Korean prison camp?" I asked.

"You would survive," she said with a note of hope.

"But if I just stopped eating, the weight would have to come off eventually," I argued, and then I came up with a brilliant strategy to force Dr. Curosh to give me appetite suppressants. "I've even been thinking about getting my stomach stapled."

SLAM DUNK. Right? I mean, stroke of brilliance. I was threatening to have parts of my body sewn shut just to lose weight. What else did she need to see how determined I was? She wouldn't have any choice now but to give me the meds.

"You know," she said, picking up her pen, "that's a very good idea."

I have since learned from Zoom that I do not have a good poker face, despite my belief that I was on top of that game, so I'm sure my eyes widened and my mouth formed a little *o*.

"It's possible to completely reverse diabetes with a gastric procedure," she said. "I would encourage you to look into it. This may be the solution for you."

That was not what I'd wanted to hear, and I felt my face get red and hot, and I really, really wanted to cry. But crying in front of someone who had just told me to get a fat operation would somehow reduce my dignity to an even lower level than it had been fifteen seconds before.

"Okay," I said, "I'll look into it."

And I did. I went to an info session at the hospital, and the surgical team confirmed what Dr. Curosh had said. I also talked to as many people as I could find who had already been through the surgery.

And that was hard, because there's a stigma attached to gastric surgery; it's often thought of as the easy way out. I knew what my obese life had been for as long as I lived it. I knew that for my body to give up any weight, I needed to be on a treadmill for two hours a day and to eat nothing but eight hundred calories worth of salad. But that is unsustainable. And with PCOS in one corner and diabetes in the other, it wasn't a fair fight.

Honestly, I didn't really give a shit what other people thought, because the only people who'd judge me were people who had never had weight issues. They'd never had a doctor poke them in the belly and say, "Stop eating Twinkies," instead of asking real questions. They'd never had a friend come up to them after they'd lost some weight by starving themselves and say, "Wow. You got really big there. I didn't know if you were ever going to get back to normal." They've never had people they've known for years ignore them at a party or not be able to meet them in the eye after a sudden forty-pound weight gain. They've never had someone look from their husband to them and say, "He's married to . . . *her*?" They've never had a salesperson in a boutique casually come up to them and whisper, "I don't think we have your size here." They've never had a close friend call and say, "I'm very worried about your health. You should try jogging."

All of those things have happened to me. And more. Ask any chubby girl what people have said to her, and it will be jaw-dropping and mortifying and soul-crushing. But I will be honest. I hated the way I looked, and I wanted to wear my old fat clothes again.

So I consulted the brilliant women whom I'd acquired as my support system over the years: my physician, my therapist, and, most importantly, my beloved former endocrinologist, Mary. Valedictorian of her medical school class, she literally fell on James Watson, one of the two men who discovered the molecular structure of DNA, as he'd handed over her diploma. Knocked him straight to the ground. Also, she'd gotten a leech in her eye while doing research in Madagascar and didn't mention it until I had known her for a decade. I mean, if I were her, I'd open with that story every time I met someone—"I got a leech in my eye when I was doing research in Madagascar. What have you got?" She's also the mother of my goddaughter, Big Al, and we do a lot of babysitting, so Mary has a vested interest in keeping me alive.

"Yes," Mary said before I even finished asking. "Your metabolism is not going to get any better without a massive scientific breakthrough. This is a great resource for you."

So I made an appointment with the surgeon and found out very quickly that this was no "easy way out."

Ahead of me would be a year of tests, procedures, lab work, counseling, and nutrition classes.

Open wide, we're going to ram a camera down your throat to see how much has been gnawed away by acid reflux. Hey, here's a bulky sleep apnea vest; we're going to strap this to your chest, and it's going to make you look like a suicide bomber. (Actual question from the technician who strapped it on me: "You didn't have plans to go to the airport tonight, did you?")

They also had me take a psych test with leading questions that I'm sure have landed my name on several watch lists.

True/False: I am well known.

TRUE (Not according to my last publisher, but every time someone looks at me naked or takes a peek at my asshole, they seem to know who I am.)

True/False: Many people do not like me.

TRUE (I have blocked roughly five hundred people on Facebook, most of whose messages began with, "As a longtime reader of yours, I'm saddened, if not actually disappointed, that (a) you support the rights of gay perverts, and I think you should go to hell; (b) you support the right of women to control their own bodies, and I think you should go to hell; and (c) you support mask mandates, and I hope you die while wearing one.")

Always/Sometimes/Rarely/Never: I hear or see things that others do not hear or see.

ALWAYS (I was walking with a friend to dinner and saw a bank robbery getaway. My friend did not believe me until the cops showed up. Also, on numerous occasions, topless women walking down the street that never seem to catch my husband's eye.)

Always/Sometimes/Rarely/Never: Others don't believe me when I tell them the things I see or hear.

ALWAYS (I heard a rock fight in my alley between two hobos. Even the cops didn't believe me. I saw one squirrel attempt to rape another squirrel, and so I threw a rock at the offending squirrel. No one believed me until I found out that I was not the first one to google "squirrel rape.")

Always/Sometimes/Rarely/Never: Do you feel that other people are watching you or talking about you?

ALWAYS (See reviews for my books on Amazon.

"This book should have been written by someone more practiced in writing historical fiction. The book settled into a quagmire of unnecessary details and seemed as though it was written for the middle school age crowd. Had to force myself to finish it." This reader has given every book I've written a review of one star.

"Very condemning of others. I've read several of her books, and I couldn't believe this one. I had to stop reading. Very rude and judgy of her to think she is so much better than others. Will not be reading any more of her books."

"Self-absorbed writer who thinks her stories should be interesting to anyone other than herself. Who ARE these reviewers who gave this book 5 stars? I'd have given it zero stars if that were an option. Don't waste your money.")

Despite the results of my psych test, my surgery finally got scheduled, and I arrived at my consult before the big day.

My surgeon was funny, from Brooklyn, and wore great shoes. She explained the procedure to me one last time and asked if I had any questions.

"I do," I said. "What do you do with the part of my stomach that you slice off?"

She paused and thought for a second. "It gets incinerated," she said, in a way that made it clear no one had ever asked her that question before. "It's biowaste."

"Has anyone ever asked to keep it?" I questioned.

"No," she said.

And then I had a very good idea.

The surgery went off without a hitch, and I was given Dilaudid again, which makes everything a lovely experience. I went home, ready to fit into my skinny-fat clothes.

I checked in with my family to let them know I had survived another surgery, and when I called my nephews, Nick and David, I told them I had a surprise for them.

"Guess what?" I said. "My stomach was so huge that they had a lot of extra bits, and there's a guy in town who can tan it like leather. So I'm making you a couple of wine pouches out of it!"

"Please don't do that, Aunt Laurie," they said in unison.

"Too late!" I replied. "Christmas is going to be really special this year. I'm going to die broke, so don't expect an inheritance, but this way you'll always have a part of me."

There was silence on the other end of the phone.

"Don't you always want to have a part of me with you?" I asked.

"I guess so," they said.

"Yay!" I said and hung up the phone. My nephews are very patient people.

I can now report the good news: my diabetes was reversed and hasn't returned. And here's the bad news: I lost some weight but not as much as I'd hoped. But it turns out that I'm cool with that. If I get to keep my kidneys, feet, and eyes, I guess I don't care how fat they are.

Six months later, I took my still-fat legs back to Phoenix for the holidays, and in my suitcase were some lovely surprises. On Christmas Eve, I put them under the tree for Nick and David, wrapped in red foil paper.

Because my nephews are now young men, there are rarely any presents waiting under the Christmas tree. In fact, we really don't do a gift exchange; it's more of a mail drop consisting of envelopes with checks inside. We don't even do this in front of the tree anymore; we just sit at the dinner table, and it takes approximately thirty seconds to hand out and complete and is as festive as an announcement that your employer is planning a reorganization.

We completed our dinner table envelope exchange. "I guess we're done then," said my mother, eager to get us all out of the house and return to her holiday baking shows. "Good night. Merry Christmas."

"No, no, no, no," I interjected. "The boys have something under the tree for them."

"We do?" Nick and David said, looking puzzled.

"YOU DO!" I exclaimed.

Curious, David went to collect the gifts and brought them back to the table.

"Open them together," I instructed.

They both tore at the red foil paper and looked puzzled when they revealed the contents.

"What is it?" David asked.

"Remember my surgery?" I asked. "They're the wine bags! Now I can be with you forever!"

Nick dropped his bag on the table. "That's gross, Aunt Laurie."

"Why is that gross?" I replied. "I got it tanned by a leather guy; it's totally fine. You wear leather shoes, don't you?"

"Not that are made out of my aunt," David said.

"Look at how nice and smooth it is!" I said, reaching across and touching the fine suede pile with my fingertip, brushing it back and forth. "I think the guy did a really nice job. I am super impressed."

"I am not drinking wine out of your stomach," David said, attempting to give the wine pouch back.

"You are being ridiculous," I said. "*Of course you're not drinking out of my stomach.* There's a plastic liner in there!"

"You are an animal," my mother said to me.

"I'm not—I can't," Nick said, shaking his head.

"I am disgusted," said their mother, my sister, Lisa. "This is disgusting."

"I don't get why you are disgusted," I said. "People get the ashes of their loved ones compressed into diamonds. I couldn't afford diamonds, but it's the same idea."

I picked up Nick's wine bag.

"Just try it once?" I asked. "I'll go first. I want to see how watertight it is."

"I don't think so," David said.

"Listen," I said sternly. "I could have had my stomach leftovers made into anything, I could have made myself a wallet or a belt, but I chose to give this to *you*. I chose to give something that was so much a part of me to you *both*. When I am gone, you will still have that wine bag to remind you of me. Because it is me. I loved you enough to do this for you. Now love me enough to just take one sip, okay?"

I picked up both wine bags, untwisted the caps, and filled them a little bit with water. I took a sip out of each and then handed them back to the boys.

"It does have that new wine bag taste," I said. "But it's perfectly fine. I have scars on my body so that I could give you this gift."

And then I just stared at them.

"It has a liner," I stressed again. "And a little plastic mouthpiece. It's perfectly sanitary."

They looked at me.

"I love you both more than life itself," I continued. "I would never give you something that would harm you. Now, please, drink from my gift. It barely smells weird."

They didn't move.

"All right, fine," I said. "Just lift it up to your mouth so that I can take a picture."

They obliged begrudgingly, and in the photo, they both look as if they are about to suckle from a filthy cow.

"I want to talk to you," my sister hissed.

I met her in the bathroom.

"You had better tell me right now if that is really your stomach," she said as soon as she shut the door.

"What do you think?" I asked.

"I think you are imbalanced enough to do that!" she replied. "Are you still seeing your shrink?"

"Of course that's not my stomach!" I said. "You can't tan an organ! You would never get a fine suede finish like the one on those bags!"

"Thank God," she said.

"It's the extra skin from my thigh when I got impaled."

"Shut up, shut up, shut up," she said, shaking her head. "I know it's not your thigh because there aren't any stretch marks on either of those bags!"

I just smiled.

"If I eventually lose enough weight," I said to her with a wink, "there might be an awesome new purse in your future."

Me and My Step-Husbands

At the exact time that I requested my husband wake me up, footsteps ascended on the stairs in his heavy-soled slippers: clomp, clomp, clomp.

The bedroom door creaked open on dry, one-hundred-year-old hinges, and on his way to my side of the bed, he stepped on one orphaned mate of a pair of Fluevogs that I got at a great sale, then tripped on a '40s rayon shirtdress that has been two sizes too small for me since the day I bought it, and occupied a nice nestling place on the floor next to the air exchange vent, where it had been collecting a fine film of dog hair.

He gently shook me, almost silently calling, "Honey, it's eight o'clock."

He waited for a moment, then another, and shook me again, urging a little louder this time, "Honey, it's time to get up."

There was no response.

He firmly gripped my shoulder, which was smothered under a down comforter, and pushed for real this time, one solid push. "It's time to get up," he said in a full voice. "It's time to get up!"

He stood back for a moment and looked carefully at my still corpse, trying to detect any movement of air—any sign of inhale, exhale—but there was none. Nothing rose, nothing fell. The comforter stayed constant in its lifeless position.

"Wake up," he urged, then said it again louder. "You need to get up!"

He turned on my dresser-top lamp and really took a steady look at his wife, my mouth open, my red lipstick smeared across my face, a smear that was mirrored across the pillowcase in a dragline from the last time I turned over. The sleeping mask only covered one eye, and the eye that was visible was closed, with no hint of REM sleep. That eye was concrete in position; it didn't flinch, flutter, or twitch.

He thought for a moment. He knew what his wife popped into her mouth at bedtime, and there was my insistence that I'm from the '90s, so my adoration for "chill pills" is unrivaled and mandated by my generation. He took a silent inventory: the pot gummies, the restless leg syndrome pill, the actual controlled-substance sleeping pill, the blue Costco pill, and the over-the-counter sleep gummies. Then he stepped on the empty ZzzQuil bottle that was peeking out from right underneath the bed. His mind immediately went to Heath Ledger. Heath Ledger, who died from a combination of sleepy-time cold medication and controlled substances. It is unknown if he, too, had restless leg syndrome.

But Ledger was *not* from the '90s.

Wait. Didn't he star in the 1999 teen comedy *10 Things I Hate About You*?

Oh shit.

"Laurie, GET UP," he said, pushing my body harder and with definite force, but that's not what made the action severe. It was the use of my name, which he never said unless he was *pissed*.

He always knew this morning would come. That he would find a colder-than-usual Laurie lying in bed and then have to deal with all of her shit. What would he do with one barely worn Fluevog and hundreds of dresses older than his mother, all accessorized with dog hair? What would he do with my collection of Inspiring Women Barbies (Who wants an Eleanor Roosevelt Barbie? Who?) and my shocking number of vintage plaid coats? There was probably another wing of our house he wasn't aware of because my shit was blocking it. My assemblage of antique books that I swore I could retire on because they "are worth something"? And all of that goddamned turquoise! Fifty pairs of cowboy boots with heels worn down to the nub on a forty-five-degree angle from the outside going in?

Not to even mention all of that stupid miniature furniture that breaks as soon as you touch it. There is a human-size room FULL of it.

"SURPRISE!" I yelled as I burst from the comforter with my arms wide open like I was a showgirl exploding from a giant birthday cake.

He stared at me for one second—cold, frozen—then bit his lip and marched out of the room and down the hall.

"I got you AGAIN!" I cackled as his footsteps got louder and deeper.

He did not respond and stomped off to another part of the house.

"It's not my fault!" I screeched. "I told you that you would never be bored if you married me!"

I didn't feel bad. I was just giving him practice for the real thing. Someday, I *will* overdose. That's a reality as much as the fact that I'm writing this right now. It will probably be an accident, and that is fine with me. It's my preferred exit.

When I expressed my acceptance of that impending death to one of my student editors at work, she burst into tears.

"I don't want you to die!" she sobbed.

"Oh, sweetheart," I said, trying to console her. "No one's ever said that to me before. Not even my mom!"

And then I gave her a dollar-an-hour raise.

And though I think my husband might feel similarly, I'm fairly sure that dread only stems from the personal-belongings disaster he stands to inherit.

I have not given him any type of raise. After that, the biggest problem my husband will encounter, then, is answering the homicide detective when they ask, "Why did you wait two weeks to call the police?"

"Because she's *done this before*," my husband will insist. "For a former smoker with lungs like a wet tissue, she can hold her breath for *a very long time*."

"But the smell," the detective would counter.

"She loves sugar-free gummy bears," I hope he will say. "The fragrance notes of those two scents are completely indistinguishable."

Sadly, he may never get that far. I fear that my husband's life expectancy will be roughly eight hours after my death. Despite opening one drawer and then trying to use the remote control to eat soup, he won't be able to find the cutlery, then give up all hope and wither away.

I have had a husband for twenty-five years, which is way longer than most successful dictatorships, and my marriage is more complicated and has more moving parts, as you can probably guess.

Truthfully, my husband is the best man in the world. Always has been. I don't know why he married me. He has tolerated—with a smile—a dozen books documenting his foibles.

203

He is, indeed, my long-suffering spouse because I am who I am—the type of wife who enjoys playing dead in bed some mornings *mostly* for my own enjoyment, and then spins it off as necessary preparation. I make no argument against my more difficult qualities. Our main dynamic hinges on the fact that my husband is not a man of annoying action, or any quick action, really; he's a questions kind of guy, and I am not an answers kind of girl. I usually avoid asking questions because I'm almost always annoyed by the answers I receive, which in the past have been things like, "Sorry, but I need you to stop what you're doing and take a picture of students on campus. I only have a flip phone." Or, "It's not a joke. Stop laughing. That *is* the copy we're using on the Instagram story." Or, "We already refunded you the charges for your overdrafts last week. We can't do it again this week, Ms. Notaro. Thank you for being the best part of Wells Fargo."

All of those answers are potential direct lines to a stroke, which I'd rather not have. I'd rather keep eating salt and stop asking questions for the sake of my health. I like to think of it as my version of preventative health care.

But my husband is an asker. He loves to start conversations with, "Where do we keep the forks?" And, "What aisle are the bananas in at Safeway?" And, "Is our ceiling supposed to look like that?"

On top of this personality type, he has an auditory reception issue, which he denies. One year for my birthday gift, I asked my husband to take a hearing test, and he claims to have passed it. I never saw any paperwork, so I don't believe it. Lie to me about an affair, and I get it; I can ignore that, plus it gives me more free time. But lie to me about hearing loss that I notice every single day? That's insanity. Because what that means is, not only do I have to tell him the bananas are in the cold part of Safeway, but I usually have to say it at least twice, pretty loudly. If he asks again, I just mouth something like, "The forks are in the cracked ceiling aisle," and wait for him to figure it out on his own instead of admitting that he can't hear properly.

Listen, ask any woman who has lived the last twenty-five years of her life on repeat if that is cruel and unusual behavior. She will tell you that no jury of her peers (women who are still married to their selective-hearing husbands after two and a half decades) would convict her. My trigger is "What?" I've lost half of the last twenty-five years to time spent being a skipping record, and at this point I do not hesitate to give dirty looks to random husbands who shoot that word to their wives like a missile in public.

Because my husband is an asker and has approximately twenty questions a day that he insists need immediate attention, I started pretending that I don't hear him and walk away, but then he took up following me until I surrendered. So I instated a household rule because one of us was going to die, either by my hand or by rope. Drastic measures needed to be taken, and immediately.

"This is the deal now," I said one morning as he began to open his mouth to ask me something, like when I thought the newspaper would be delivered, or where his dirty laundry bag might be, or if it was recycling or lawn-trimming pickup that week. "You get one free question a day. One. Any questions after that, I charge a dollar per answer. Three dollars for an answer I have to repeat. Do you understand?"

"Why?" he asked.

This is the reason we don't keep weapons in the house.

"Do you really want to use your free question for something that's going to end up costing you hundreds by the end of the day?" I replied. "Don't ask why. Just say, 'Okay.'"

"Can I say that I think it's unfair?" he dared.

"No, and with that, sir, you have just used your complimentary question," I said as I went downstairs to the basement to bang my head on the concrete. "Have fun figuring out what the Netflix password is. I'll give you a hint: you picked it."

Like a cub who follows a male lion that is not his father, my husband was foolishly on my heels with every step as I made my escape.

"But—" he started. "I need to run errands today. When does the bank open? Does Safeway still carry almond milk? Have you seen my Vans? Does Maeby need chicken treats? And where is the bank?"

I do believe I had an aneurysm at that point, but the next contact my skull made with the wall sealed it right back shut again.

I stopped for a moment and tried to draw a breath.

"Wendy, darling, light of my life," I said through clenched teeth and a full Jack Nicholson grin. "I don't know, I don't know, I don't know."

"Could I get a discount on those answers?" he asked. "They weren't very helpful."

"GET. BACK. UPSTAIRS," I replied, pointing, then realized he needed bait. "Your Vans are on the bathroom floor on top of your dirty laundry bag next to your newspaper."

When I heard him close the basement door, I erupted.

"What time does the bank open?" I hissed in a whisper of fire, hunched over like Gollum. *"Am I the bank psychic? I am not the keeper of the bank! Of course Safeway carries almond milk! Are almonds an endangered nut? Why would Safeway not have almond milk? Is there an almond milk embargo? Just drink regular milk like every other normal person on earth. My God. Friggin' almond milk. It looks like filthy bathwater. STOP ASKING ME QUESTIONS! Google it like a grown-up. What time does the bank open? Google it! Is there an almond milk embargo? GOOGLE IT! I can't take it anymore! Where is the bank? Drive around until you find it. What am I, the Wizard of Oz???"*

I paused to catch my breath to go into Tirade, Act Two, when I heard a voice from another floor in our house say, "You know, I can HEAR YOU!"

❧

Suffice it to say that if my husband does not know where the bank is, he is a gentleman husband, which has the same meaning as a gentleman farmer. The guy who owns the land but couldn't pull a plow upon threat of death by emasculation. He'd simply have an endless well of questions before taking any of the household tasks on. I have tried to solve this problem by either doing things myself, letting things go until he notices them, or hiring an unhoused person seeking work, which was successful until he came home one day and found a fellow in our palm tree, tangled up in an electrical cord that was pulled into a very active chain saw.

And though it's a great story he likes to tell at cocktail parties when I am in another room, he always leaves out the part that the reason there was a homeless guy in our tree taking swipes at leaves and our roof with a murder weapon was because my husband had neglected to do it—ever—and we had just received a notice from the city that we were facing a fine.

I'm going to say right now that I don't care what anyone says about gender roles or if anyone questions why I didn't get my own ass up in that tree. I didn't get up in that tree because I laid the tile on the porch, I stripped the lead paint off the fireplace, I built the raised garden bed, I reglazed the antique house windows with putty, I laid the brick terrace floor, and I built a river rock wall in the front yard. My husband came home and all of these things were already done. No questions asked.

I didn't get up in that tree because I didn't fucking want to, and I'm tired.

I had the same feeling last year, when I looked over my backyard and saw hundreds of pounds of dead leaves—soggy, decaying, and full of water—layering every single square foot. I didn't want to rake them up. And I realized that the only way to get it done was to begin a relationship with another, more answer-inclined man.

I found Shawn on Facebook Marketplace; he was a young man with the strength of a stallion and the endurance of Pa Ingalls. I didn't even need to see a picture or know what his hobbies were. All I needed to know was that he had a hauling trailer and a rake.

And the next day, when he pulled into my driveway and told me he charged thirty dollars an hour, I had no idea how complete my life would become.

For ninety bucks, Shawn—rugged, forceful, amazing Shawn—left that backyard so clean I didn't even know we had trees.

As I sent over the money via Venmo, I got a little brave. "What else do you do?" I asked, batting what eyelashes I have left.

"Oh, anything you want," he said. "Landscaping, hauling, anything like that."

I felt flush with hope. The future I saw for myself was possible for thirty dollars an hour.

"I have two hydrangeas and a bum knee," I said, pointing to the nearly dead plants my husband had promised to plant a month before.

"Sure," Shawn said with joy. "I can do that right now while I have an actual tool for gardening in my hand."

My eyes went moist and fawn-like. I heard an angel sing. Or it might have been Shawn.

"I loooooov—" I whispered, suddenly stopping myself. "I'd love that."

Every month, I'd get butterflies in my stomach making a list of things I needed Shawn to do. It was like Christmas every four weeks. Trim the laurels. Chop the rhodies. Eviscerate those blackberries! Dig up that volunteer tree that landed in the wrong place. Clear out that awful side planter of brambles; let's plant hostas instead! For every task, he showed up, ready to complete the assignment, no questions asked.

Then the day came—as I knew it would. I had seen an antique cupboard on Facebook Marketplace—a site that is like an opium den for people who appreciate cheap antiques—and since Shawn had fetched other treasures for me with his trailer, I called to ask when he was available. But Shawn had become such a popular step-husband that he was booked out for weeks.

"Oh," I said, devastated. "I told them I could pick it up this weekend."

"I have a friend with a truck," he said. "He loves to do things like that. Let me give him a call."

And that is how I met my second step-husband, Jeremiah, who was actually Shawn's almost-stepbrother. Jeremiah's dad and Shawn's mom had dated for years, and the two boys had grown up together.

Jeremiah was also thirty dollars an hour, but he would go anywhere to pick up stuff for me, and because I was getting my fix on Facebook Marketplace every day, I saw him a lot. He picked up a primitive hutch for me in Turner, Oregon. He wrestled a two-hundred-pound 1940s washing machine from three hours away and another antique washing machine from Albany to my backyard. He fetched an antique cast-iron bed from Draperville, a 1950s metal glider from Portland, and antique wavy-glass windows from every nook and cranny in the state. And he collected several old farmhouse doors from an architectural salvage place. I even met his grandma Pearl and gave her a tomato plant. He was at my house so much that my mailman asked me if I had gotten remarried.

"Kind of," I replied.

"I could tell," he said, smiling. "You're glowing."

Jeremiah started bringing over things he thought I would like.

"I found this old door at a friend's house," he said one summer Wednesday. "They were going to burn it!"

"That's a four-paneled Doug fir door with original hardware," I said. "I'll Venmo you thirty dollars right now!"

The backyard was getting crowded with old things from around the state, and that's when I called in my next step-husband, Kregg. He had already built a bookcase upstairs and renovated my bathroom, so he was very well aware that I am a little bit insane. He saw the backyard full of doors, cabinets, and washing machines.

"Oh my God," he said slowly. "Are you building a rocket?" Kregg is a man of both action and questions. I can live with that.

"NO!" I said cheerfully. "You're building me a studio!"

"With these old windows and doors?" he asked, wincing.

"YES!" I almost screamed. "Isn't it awesome?"

Kregg has the steadiest poker face on the planet. Don't ever involve yourself in a card game with him. You will lose everything you've ever worked for.

"Yes," he said calmly.

It was Kregg who hauled in two-hundred-year-old fir floor planks from a lady in Veneta and installed a seven-foot-tall stained-glass window that came out of a house down the street (don't ask how I got it). No one would do that for a woman unless he loved her, or she was paying him by the hour. Personally, I prefer the latter arrangement, being that I don't have to hear about his painful pinky toe, blocked left sinus, or the fact that he has five meetings scheduled that day before I even launch myself out of REM sleep.

"What are you going to do with the washing machines?" he asked. "Are you starting a laundry business?"

"Step-husband number three, it's like you don't know me at all," I protested. "Those are planters for the garden we're going to build next to the greenhouse with antique windows that is in Studio Phase 4b."

"Great," he said with no expression at all.

"How can you not know me better than that?" I lamented. "We built a bathroom together with marble penny tile in an intricate pattern."

"Oh, I remember," he said. "I remember that I laid the tile, and you told me how to lay the tile."

I smiled.

"We will always have that," I said fondly. "Always."

"I won't forget," he added. "Ever."

My fourth step-husband is arguably my most valuable player, but I hadn't seen him or thought about him much until my drain clogged last week and I needed a superhero, as my legal husband sadly watched a dam gurgling out of the P trap under our sink and asked aloud, "Is that water?"

"It's clear and wet," I said with my magnificent powers of observation, pulling out my cell phone.

"Yo," John, my plumber, said. "Better not be shit balls again, Notaro."

There are four things you need to notice in that above sentence:

1. I am a named contact on a plumber's phone.
2. He calls me by my dude name.
3. He knows my biggest fear: shit balls—aberrations of nature that commonly appear in our basement when the roots of centuries-old trees get tangled in our sewer and clog it up. (On their inaugural appearance, my husband mistook them for mud balls and carefully saved them to show John in case they would be a key to solving the puzzle of the clogged sewer. Can't say he wasn't right.)
4. THE MOST IMPORTANT OF ALL: he answers my calls.

When's the last time a man who drilled through your poo with a power tool answered your call? Exactly.

John gets me out of approximately five disasters a year, which qualifies him for the Rock hero status. We work so well together that I've almost suggested we heist a bank.

"You can't rob a bank with John!" my husband laughed at me once in the middle of a fight. "You can't even run! The only quality a criminal must have is the ability to escape. You'd need a stand-in."

"Maybe true, but my point was that I *can* get along with other people," I protested. "Plus, I've never ruled out the possibility of robbing a bank on skates."

I don't know if my original husband is jealous of my other husbands, but when I asked him point-blank, he replied, "I don't even know what you're talking about, but it's just more ways to prove that I am inadequate."

I wanted to say, "Then let's sign you up for carpentry, plumbing, and digging classes with the time you spend watching reruns of *Veronica Mars*," but I didn't because at that moment we both suspected I had given him COVID, so the timing was not the best.

What I *did* learn from having step-husbands is that once you've secured a nice collection of them, you must be selfish. I learned this all too well when I called Shawn to schedule a date and, for the second time, he broke the news that he was booked up for the next two months.

"Booked up?!" I gasped. "With what? With *who*?"

"Well, I'm working on several ladies' lawn renos," he explained. "And George has me blocked out for a full week to work on all of the things around his house."

"George?" I asked. "George, my boss?"

"Yes, George your boss, who you kissed," Shawn said.

"I don't want to talk about that right now, but he booked you for a week?" I asked. "Like a Vegas act? Like, are you moving in?"

Shawn laughed nervously. "Um, no," he said.

"I didn't know you were available for long-term commitments," I replied gruffly.

"You never asked," he responded.

"Then I want you for the whole week after George," I demanded.

"I don't think I have a whole week—no, I don't," he said. "I'm at Mrs. Murez's house, then Mrs. Wheeler's house."

"Who is Mrs. Murez?" I almost screamed. "Who is Mrs. Wheeler?"

"Well, they are George's neighbors," he coughed up.

George was passing out the details of *my* step-husband, the one I found, to all of his lady friends with lame original husbands, like he was some pool boy. That was an outrage. I found Shawn, *I did*, sitting on the curb of Facebook and Marketplace, practically begging for work. I discovered him. I shone a light on him. I made him a commodity. And I gave his number to George.

It was all my fault. He was just a guy with a trailer when I met him. Then, with one leak of his phone number, one little mistake, my whole lawn relationship was in jeopardy.

AND, I wanted to know, why does George need a step-husband? But then I quickly remembered that several weeks prior, his wife had gone out of town, and he had gone skiing alone. During that trip, he ate it on his first pass down the mountain, and despite his foot throbbing in pain, he decided to go up for another pass. Then he hobbled to his car and drove two hours to the closest emergency room, where they told George he had broken his foot.

What George actually needed, I suspected, was a pair of crutches and his wife with him at all times.

I resolved to keep the remainder of my step-husbands close, not revealing their identities to anyone who needed a furniture-getter, a carpenter, or, God forbid, a plumber. I'm not getting stuck with mud balls scattered all over my basement for a week because I bragged about the location of my golden treasure named John.

The day came when my husband clomped up the stairs from the basement, out of breath from both fury and disgust.

"Honey," he said, huffing, "you need to call John again. The mud balls are back."

"Oh, I don't know about that," I said. "I wouldn't want to make you feel inadequate, you know. You sure you don't want to give it a shot first?"

He looked at me in frozen horror, a million questions bouncing around like pinballs inside his brain.

"Oh, I'm just joking! I'm not that mean," I said. "But you could find yourself a nice step-wife to call him."

Don't Call It a Crisis

I needed a car.

I only needed a car.

For more than fifteen years, my husband and I had owned only one car. We both worked within walking distance from our house, and we lived in a small town. I could see the cinder blocks of a Safeway from my window, and anywhere else we typically went, we went together.

That was, until my friend Amy rented a house on the Oregon coast last summer and asked me to come out to visit her for a week. I was game, naturally, and as I wheeled my suitcase out to the car the morning of my departure, my husband looked puzzled standing there to say goodbye.

"Wait," he said instead, looking at the car and then me. "You're taking the Prius?"

"No," I replied. "I cashed out our 401(k)s to pay for a cab to the coast. Yes, I'm taking the Prius. How else did you think I'd get there?"

"I don't know," my husband replied. "I thought maybe you were . . . renting a car?"

I entered into a contract over a quarter of a century ago to marry this man and to spend the rest of my life choosing not to kill him.

I took a deep breath and tried to control my strangle-hand.

"Why would I rent a car," I said, pausing for effect, "when I already own one?"

"How—" my husband began before I cut him off.

"Look! There's a lady struggling with getting a ten-pound bag of potatoes into her car right now in the parking lot of the grocery store," I said, pointing. "But I can't see Amy. Or her beach house. For this week, you will get to the store by using your feet. That's how. And I am going to drive the one hundred fifty miles to my vacation."

"Almond milk is heavy," he protested.

"Then get it delivered," I replied. And then I put my suitcase in the car and left.

I called to check in every night and see what kind of disaster my husband had found himself in that day.

"The new Spider-Man movie was playing at ten this morning, and I would have had the whole theater by myself," he told me one night. "But I couldn't get there."

"My friends invited me to happy hour at the new drinky place downtown," he said. "I stayed home instead and made a cocktail with diet cranberry ginger ale, Kahlúa, and an apple. It was all we had in the house. I called it a Laurie Has the Car."

"Maeby wanted to go for a car ride, but I couldn't fit her in the basket on my bike," he told me another night. "You should see how sad she is."

I hung up the phone without replying that third night and stared at Amy in disbelief.

"You would think I left that man stranded on an island with a volleyball for company," I said in a huff.

"How have you lived for that long with only one car?" she asked.

"Because I can drive from one end of town to the other faster than I can get a bacon, egg, and cheese biscuit at McDonald's on a Saturday morning," I said. "I tried to get lost in our town once but ended up driving past my house seven times. I finally gave up and pulled into the driveway on the eighth pass."

"Maybe you just need your own car," Amy said.

"You know," I said, nodding enthusiastically, "maybe I do!"

"What would you get?" Amy asked eagerly.

"I have no idea," I said. I'd never thought about it. When we bought the Prius, it was the responsible choice. Was it the car of my dreams? No. It was just a responsible decision. I'd wanted a turquoise 1965 Nash convertible in high school.

Instead, I got a Chevy Citation, which was about an inch longer than a Pinto, and I didn't complain. It had a red velour interior that I thought looked regal, but the transmission blew within six months and left me and two friends stranded in the desert near a town called Picacho that wasn't much more than a gas station and a phone booth.

Over the next thirty years, I drove a long line of sensible cars, including every midsize Toyota and Honda ever made. I was never a "car person." But looking at Amy, I started to smile.

"I could get a fun car," I said.

"You will get a fun car," she confirmed.

"I could get something sporty," I added.

"You could get a convertible," she said.

I gasped, thinking back to high school reveries of the Nash.

Why *couldn't* I get one? I could pay for my own car. I had good insurance, plus I apparently needed a car.

"I'm going to get a car as soon as I get back!" I announced to Amy.

And as soon as I got home, I told my husband that his car troubles were over.

"I'm getting my own car," I told him. "I'm getting a convertible."

"Oh," he said, looking shocked. "A midlife crisis car?"

"Let me remind you who in this house had a crisis because they didn't have a car for a couple of days," I said.

"Just because I'm going to get a convertible doesn't mean it's a midlife crisis car."

"Yes, it does," he replied.

I looked at used cars online for a week before I found the Nash. It wasn't a convertible, but it *was* turquoise. I showed it to my first-place step-husband, Shawn, when he was over doing yard work.

"Do you know how to work on cars?" he asked. "It's a beautiful car, but it will be in the shop all the time. They don't make parts for that anymore."

I was bummed, but he had a point. "What about an MG, or a Karmann Ghia, something like that?" I asked him, but he still had concerns.

"You really need a newer car," he advised me. "Something with a paint job that will hold up in Oregon weather."

He was right. Twenty, thirty, forty years ago, someone huffed and puffed and blew what would have been my garage down to build a garden. And I couldn't be the one to ruin a classic car with inevitable rust and moss. Because moss does, indeed, grow inside cars in Oregon.

"What about a MINI Cooper?" he asked. "I think that would check all of your boxes. And you wouldn't have to keep it in a garage."

"Shawn," I said to the man I paid thirty dollars an hour to be my husband, "do you think it's a midlife crisis car?"

"Of course not," he said, making thirty-five cents as he answered. "What makes you think that?"

"Because I'm middle-aged," I said, knowing that launching this information onto my twenty-eight-year-old step-husband would change his view of me forever, being that I easily present to the world as thirty years younger.

But he didn't flinch, which was surprising.

"Mrs. Notaro," he said, "if it's the car you want and you like, get it. You should be able to drive whatever car you want. *It's your car.*"

Shawn was right. A MINI Cooper certainly wasn't a statement car like a Tesla, a Hummer, or an Escalade. It was just a tiny little car to tool around town in.

But when I told my IRL husband that I thought I had found the one I wanted on Facebook Marketplace—a cute two-door silver convertible for a very reasonable price—and showed it to him, he blatantly laughed.

"Here's to you, Mrs. Robinson," he sang. "You really are going all the way, aren't you?"

"Stop it," I said. "It's just a car."

"A midlife crisis car," he shot back.

"You know," I answered flatly, "I didn't flinch when you started keeping a journal because you said your life 'was slipping through your fingers like sand on a forgotten beach.' I didn't say anything when you started collecting fountain pens and then spent hours listening to fountain pen podcasts and making jokes about 'nibs.' I never said anything. And I didn't call it a crisis."

"I think when your favorite purchase of the last decade was fold-up TV trays, you're at that point to qualify," my husband said.

"Oh my God!" I screamed. "You take advantage of that purchase every single night and enjoy it every bit as much as I do!"

"At least I took the plastic covering off mine!" he retorted.

"I told you that I was not taking the manufacturer's protective film off until we had a noteworthy guest over," I said. "A scratched TV tray is a sad TV tray. What does that say to people?"

"It says you are serving people dinner like it was Meals on Wheels," he said. "I think dessert should start coming with an Epsom salt footbath."

"Okay, well, you know how you ate all of those beef jerky treats on vacation and said there was no taste to them?" I asked.

"Yes, and I've told you not to buy them again," he replied.

"Well, I did!" I exclaimed. "Because they were for the *dog*! It said so right on the bag, but you didn't have your glasses on and didn't see it before you ate all of them and threw the bag away."

"Okay, well, I have news for you," he said, putting his hands on his hips. "Remember when you said that ever since you were a little girl you had a 'gummy smile' and you were so happy now that your teeth have grown so you don't have that much gum showing?"

"I have a beautiful smile now!" I yelled.

"It's GINGIVITIS!" he replied. "Your gums are receding! Your teeth aren't growing!"

That one hurt.

I gasped. "Long . . . in the tooth?" I whispered to myself.

Then I did the only thing I could do. I messaged the owner of the MINI Cooper and made an appointment to see it the next day.

That night, I went to happy hour with some girlfriends and told them about the car.

"Oh, I looooove those," my friend Jen said. "One time I was at Target loading all of my stuff into the back of my SUV when a lady parked next to me in a MINI. I guess I stopped what I was doing and just stared, I was so jealous. I was in sweats, hair in a ponytail, and my kids were screaming. Then the lady got out. She had long silver hair, very glamorous, and she stopped when she saw me. I realized I was staring, but she smiled and said, 'One day, you'll have one of these too. And you will have earned it.'"

The next day, I bought a MINI Cooper. I saw it, drove it down the street like an old lady driving someone else's car, and fell in love. I didn't even bargain. If anything went wrong, I figured at the very least I could sic my father on the seller. My dad, I reasoned, would be all too eager, given the new hobby he'd developed since he retired. He had become a telemarketer stalker, eagerly picking up every call that came through his phone. He waited for the telemarketer to deliver his spiel and then attacked.

"You know, guy, I don't know who you think you called, but you called *me*," he would inform the telemarketer in his Brooklyn accent. "And I know a guy who knows a guy who knows a guy who could make it very scary for you to start your car tomorrow morning. So, if I were you, I'd really take a look at the last name of the person you are about to call. Because if you call N-O-T-A-R-O again, it will be your last mistake. You got me?"

On the rare occasions when he missed a telemarketer's call, he would present with an intense melancholy, but would make up for it with delight if he was able to successfully hit "return call" and launch into his hobby once again. It was enough to scare anybody. If I had bought a lemon, I was sure my dad would make gallons of lemonade with it.

My husband came with me the next week to pick up the car, and as I drove it back down I-5 toward Eugene, I didn't feel like I had earned it. I even put a Hole CD in to make the inaugural drive memorable, thinking I would scream-sing the whole way home with Courtney Love. But instead I felt like Mrs. Robinson, with my long teeth and TV trays, and barely mumbled, "I'm Miss World, somebody kill me . . ." The whole thing was sad. My husband followed behind me in the Prius, and when we parked the cars, he came over to the MINI.

"What's the matter?" he asked. "You didn't even put the top down."

I shrugged. "I really did feel like an old lady in her midlife crisis car," I admitted. "I felt stupid."

"I'm really sorry," my husband said, putting his arm around me. "I took that too far. I think I was still stinging from not getting one laugh from you on my nib jokes. I really hurt your feelings."

"It's all right," I replied. "I just wanted something fun, and it turns out it wasn't all that fun after all. It's just a car."

"It is *not* just a car," my husband answered. "Are you kidding me? You were the cutest car on the road! Everyone was jealous! Even I could see that driving behind you!"

"You're lying," I said.

"I'm not," he said as he headed toward the house. "I'll prove it to you. Start the car. Put the top down."

So I did, and a minute later he came out with Maeby, our 1,500-year-old dog, and put her in the back seat. He jumped in the passenger seat and pointed.

"Let's go for a drive," he instructed.

I headed up the hill and drove for three minutes before I hit the outskirts of town, which led into the swirly, sweeping roads of Oregon's wine country.

The sun was a soft yellow but bright; it was an uncharacteristically warm October day. I swept through the fir trees and entered a valley that was dotted with fall colors.

"Go faster," my husband said, pointing at my thirty-five-mile-per-hour speed.

I hit the gas to reach forty-five, and the sun, it seemed, dared us to chase it. My hair was flying, but the breeze was mild and made me laugh. Maeby even popped her head out of the car to catch the wind in her jowls. The Oregon countryside is exquisite any time of year, but on this October day, it seemed like it was blazing with color, fresh air, and the crisp smell of fall.

"Go FASTER," my husband insisted, and that's when I turned to him and said, "Do you want to drive?"

"YES!!!" he yelled, and I pulled over and we switched places.

He took that car to fifty in about three seconds and then shook his head. "Something's missing!" he yelled over the wind and reached forward to turn up the stereo.

"I MADE MY BED, I'LL LIE IN IT, I MADE MY BED, I'LL DIE IN IT," Courtney Love, who is one year older than I am, screamed.

"SING!" my husband commanded. And I did as I was told, at the top of my lungs.

It was SO. MUCH. FUN.

"Oh my God!" I screamed when the song ended. "I am so happy!"

My husband laughed. It was one of the best days we had ever had, zipping around the Willamette Valley, in and out of the sunshine, past farms, vineyards, and small, quaint towns. We were going to remember this for a long, long time.

"This is not a midlife crisis car," I corrected him. "This is a midlife memory car!"

From the oncoming direction, a car approached, another convertible enjoying the drive, and the grayhairs in that car waved as we passed them. We waved back.

We had earned it.

My Darling Girl

"I can come over in the afternoon," the vet said on the voice message. "I'll need four hundred dollars, cash or check."

I looked at my husband as I turned off the speakerphone, not believing what I had just heard.

"I know vets have to have composure of steel," I said. "But four hundred bucks in cash to put a dog to sleep is not the bedside manner I was hoping for."

Our dog, Maeby, was old. It wasn't like we weren't expecting this. Ten months earlier, our regular vet had given her weeks to live after discovering that her cancer had returned, this time as a tumor on her spleen.

But Mae hadn't seemed to notice. She still bounded up and down the stairs, went for two walks a day, and barked fiercely at anything that moved in front of our house. She was still old Mae, but just a little bit older. I identified with her fiercely.

She had escaped death more times than all the members of Mötley Crüe combined. Four times I'd been told that she wouldn't be with us for much longer, and to prepare for the worst. Each time, she surprised us by beating the odds, whether it was her diagnosis of lupus; a deep, rumbling case of pneumonia; a stroke; or a cancerous tumor on her liver that she had a 2 percent chance of surviving after surgery.

"The cancer will return," the surgeon advised us. "But it's so slow growing that she'll pass from something else before it's an issue."

She'd pulled through every time, even living long enough for the cancer to return. The iron will of a little dog who came from the pound. She and her littermates had been abandoned in a cardboard box behind a library in a town five miles from us, a town that has now been burned to the ground by wildfires. And I don't mean that the library burned down; the entire town did. It is completely gone. I hate that person who left her behind, and I love that person in equal measure: How could someone abandon six-week-old puppies outside in Oregon? By the same hand, I'm so glad that they did.

Suffice it to say that I don't drive a nice car; my older-model Prius is beat up and dirty and smells like a zebra pen at the zoo. Maeby is and has always been my Lexus, because veterinary surgeries aren't cheap.

And neither, apparently, was the last medical procedure of all that the vet would provide.

Only days earlier, Mae had been fine—barking, throwing temper tantrums, and being her usual self—until one morning when she just couldn't seem to wake up. She was lethargic and wouldn't eat, drink, or even get up. She was also coughing, which was not surprising, given that she had been previously diagnosed with something actually called "old dog lung."

I called our vet—I only have to say "Maeby" and they know who I am—and brought her in. We left with a bottle of strong antibiotics and a $1,200 bill for X-rays and blood tests, knowing that she'd be better in a couple of days and that the expense was worth it.

But she wasn't. The next day, she was worse, not even lifting her head. I called the vet again, and fearing that she was having a reaction to the meds, the vet prescribed a different antibiotic that wasn't as potent.

But Mae was sinking deeper and deeper. I called out of work. Dripping Pedialyte into her mouth with a dropper, I was afraid that she wouldn't pull out of it this time. By the next day, she wouldn't even swallow the liquid; it just flowed out the other side of her mouth and made a puddle.

I called the vet again and told her that I was afraid we had reached a point where we had to make a decision. She agreed, and I asked her if she would come to our house and help us out, so to speak. I knew she didn't make house calls, but I was hoping that she'd make an exception, having been Mae's vet since Mae was a baby.

But she said that she couldn't and instead gave me the name of a mobile vet who would make house calls for euthanasia.

I waited for a while before I called, hoping that Mae would perk up, or that the drugs would start working and she'd pull out of it once again. But if not for the slight movement of her chest up and down, I would have thought she had already gone.

After half an hour of watching her, I picked up the phone and left a message for the mobile vet that explained what I needed.

After I hung up, I just felt sick. Overwhelming dread. Regret. So much so that I didn't even answer the call when the mobile vet called back; I just let it go to voice mail.

When I played it back, I put it on speakerphone so that my husband could hear.

"I can come over in the afternoon," she said. "I'll need four hundred dollars, cash or check."

"Oh my God," I said to him. "Cash or check? It's like we just put a hit out on Maeby. That's insane. It's not like she even has to track Mae down or trail her. She's right here! Four hundred dollars to come over and stick a needle into a little dog who won't even resist?"

"I don't like the feel of this," my husband said. "And we don't even have that much in cash right now."

That was true. Having just given $1,200 to our regular vet, we were drained.

We talked it over. Mae was peaceful, not in any apparent pain. She was just sleeping, her hairy little belly moving up and down with each breath. If she was suffering, that would be a different story; I would have gone next door to borrow $400 from my neighbor. If they'd said no, I would have robbed them. But that wasn't the case. She wasn't in any distress. I gave her more Pedialyte, and this time she swallowed it. I crushed her antibiotic and mixed it in with the liquid, and she took that too.

We decided that we couldn't make the call. That if Mae was not suffering, we were going to let her go when it was her time.

I called the vet assassin back. Thankfully, she didn't answer.

"Thank you so much," I said, leaving a message. "But I think we're going to go in another direction. Our dog is not in distress; she's just sleeping. We're going to let her go the *Little House on the Prairie* way. Should our situation change, I'll be in touch."

I hung up the phone and looked at my husband.

"The *Little House on the Prairie* way?" he questioned. "She probably thinks we're going to shoot Mae."

"Pa never shot anybody," I argued. "Everyone knows that!"

We sat by Mae the entire day, giving her Pedialyte and Ensure with her meds mixed in. Before sunset, she lifted her head, and then she tried to get up. My husband picked her up and took her outside, where she did her business.

Then she took more Ensure, and by the morning, she was able to walk outside on her own. In two days, she was back to normal. Mae, it seemed, had more lives than Shirley MacLaine.

She had dodged another bullet.

That was almost a year ago. Before she got sick, we took her on her "last" beach vacation and marveled at every little thing she did, even telling her to say goodbye to the ocean. We are now heading out to the coast again, a year later.

She can hear a little less; she can see a little less. One tap on the fanny means "go," and two taps mean "stop," because she can no longer hear me when I say those commands. When I walk her outside, I do so with my hand on her back because she needs to know that I am there.

She needs me more now than she did when she was a puppy. Either by preference or need, she refuses to eat except when it's out of our hands. She's also taken to being finicky, only eating jarred baby food for lunch and a bottle of Ensure for dinner. The latter is administered with a twenty-milliliter syringe through a gaping hole in her jaw left from a tooth extraction that came in at three grand (one thousand for every extra root). It was the best three grand I ever spent, as that gap is what has enabled us to sustain her weight for the entirety of last year.

The vet marvels.

"I don't know how she's kept that weight on," she said to me.

"I feed Maeby like a suffragette," I answered. "One way or another, it's going down, Alice Paul."

The vet smiles. She doesn't get my jokes.

Maeby is still costly, and still the reason why I don't drive a Lexus. My beat-up Prius is just fine. When our vet recently remodeled their office, I was secretly hoping that there would be a brass plate on the wall stating, "Renovation underwritten by Maeby Notaro," because I know we paid for a chunk of it.

For what it's worth, they are always startled and happily surprised when I call and ask for an appointment; it's their sign of life that their benefactor is still showing up to work.

She is a remarkable being. She is the most perfect thing ever born. She is the love of my life. And she is going to die soon.

I can't be foolish and think I have another year with her, although I'm both excited at the prospect of saying my dog is seventeen, eighteen, and terrified of what that might look like. She has been politely banned from the groomer's; the possibility of her dropping dead while in the middle of a cut and blow-dry is admittedly high. As a result, her nails belong to Janet Jackson, and she has developed the shaggy, mottled coat of a coyote, despite my daily attempt to brush her.

But with those cosmetic losses comes a new brand of freedom for her; when she barks, she is no longer shushed. Given her old dog lung, we see it as exercise, and her shouting at the world, "I AM MAEBY, AND I AM ALIVE!"

If she would rather pee in the front yard like a trashy dog instead of heading down the back steps, we let her. Our lawn is a Jackson Pollock version of *Maeby Was Here*, flourished with spots and trails of dead grass that have recorded her biological maneuvers.

We wrap her pills with butter. I make her bacon several times a week. She can have anything she wants if these, indeed, are some of her last days. I also wonder why I ever denied her anything when she has brought nothing but joy and elation into our lives.

I watch her as she picks the green beans that I've cooked for her out of her food and spits them onto the floor, and I get it. I've taken that as a cue when advancing into my own second (or third) act. There's no time for shit you don't like.

Mae doesn't like green beans. I don't like fish. I don't like assholes. I don't like wasting time. I don't want to waste any more of it.

My time with this amazing, beautiful creature is finite. We have an end date. It is coming sooner than I want.

"You are the best thing ever born," I tell her as I hug her completely. "We are so happy we have you."

There are close calls, times when I see her snoozing on the deck in a perfect bathing sun, and there is no movement, and I'm about to call for my husband when her ear twitches, or her paws start running in her dream.

And if I'm honest, if I'm brutally honest, I am hoping that one day I walk out onto the deck and the ears don't twitch, and the paws don't run, and she has slipped away while galloping in some meadow, and never looks back to see where I am. She just keeps running.

Because she deserves a serene, easy death. I want to be able to give that to her—something so quiet and flawless, it goes like a whisper, and just like that, it's done, it's complete. No calls to the vet, no knowing the assassin is on their way, no wrenching nausea and wondering forever if I've done the right thing. No needles. Just a drifting away.

She doesn't know that she's old, or how close she is to not being with us anymore. But I do, and I'm terrified. Absolutely terrified. I push that thought as far from me as I can, but it waits just shy of my peripheral vision. It would be magical if we could accept loss and move on in the next minute, but grief must fall on one of us, and I'd rather take it than hand it to her.

There are two old ladies living in my house, and neither one of us can figure out how we got here. One lives in a quiet, blurry fog, and the other watches, hoping that she can stretch time, wield it in some way that is impossible. She is also so thankful that we've been able to grow old and older together, determined to soak up every bit of joy, mayhem, and love in every day we have left.

Acknowledgments

I humbly ask forgiveness to the following people for exposing the details of their private lives.

My husband and our beautiful girl, Maeby, my sisters, parents, Nick, David, and Reeve, Amy Silverman and her wonderful family, Meg Halverson, Colleen Feeney, Bruce Tracy, Bruce Tracy, Bruce Tracy, David Dunton, Laura Greenberg, the Upton family, Judy McDonald, Jamie Schroeder, Jeff Abbott, Mary and Bennet Smith, Big Al, Ellyn Allison, Lore Carrillo, Tee Rivers, Kim Vee, Chrissy Supah8, Angela Lindig, Michelle Loyet, Michelle Jennings, Teri Queen, Nancy Ragghanti, Cindy Dach, Beth Pearson, Deb Johnson Nies, Jen Lancaster, Quinn Cummings, Marlitt Dellabough, Melody Leslie, Lesil Larson, Shar Nelson, Libby McQuire, Julia Sommerfield, Laura Van der Veer, Emma Reh, Sara Cina, Sandra Quihas, Jim Swafford and his seventeen-page letters to Oracle and Cox Cable, Karen Ford, John Smith, Shawn Lindahl, Jeremiah Williams, Kregg

Zellner, Sebastiane Power, Sara Loveless, Mark Mueller, the Mueller kids, the Tryk family, Louise Bishop and Jim Earl, Deb Johnson Nies, Ryan Thiess, Paula Braswell, Barbara Mossberg, Casey Shoop, everyone at Little A who have been awesome beyond belief. To my poor (and exceptional) bosses, who never know what to do with me but trust me anyhow: Tobin Klinger, George Evano, Gabe Paquette, Jennifer Lindsey.

Thank you to all of the readers, especially my gang on FB. You make me laugh, smile, or spit out my drink every single day.

To the memories of Lawrence Zubia, Doug Hopkins, Dick Vonier, Chuck Bowden, all essential stars in the sky of my youth.

And to my wonderful communications team at CHC, my kids—I love you so! I cannot wait to see what good you do in this world.

To the people who have said no to me or just dropped me like a hot potato. All that does is make me work harder (and I have put curses on you all).

Most of all to you if you are still reading: I really hope we get to do this again. Thank you for sticking with me.

Cue music.

Love,

Laurie

About the Author

Photo © 2021 Laurie Notaro

Laurie Notaro is the #1 *New York Times* bestselling author of the humor memoirs *The Idiot Girls' Action-Adventure Club*, *Autobiography of a Fat Bride*, *I Love Everybody*, *The Idiot Girl and the Flaming Tantrum of Death*, a finalist for the Thurber Prize, and *Housebroken*, among others. She is also the author of three works of fiction, including the historical novel *Crossing the Horizon*. Born in Brooklyn, New York, she then spent the remainder of her formative years in Phoenix, Arizona, where she created something of a checkered past. Laurie now resides in Eugene, Oregon, has a cute dog and a nice husband, and misses Mexican food like it was her youth.